"The Spirit of Party"

"The Spirit of Party"

HAMILTON & JEFFERSON AT ODDS

MARGARET C. S. CHRISTMAN

PUBLISHED BY THE
NATIONAL PORTRAIT GALLERY
SMITHSONIAN INSTITUTION
WASHINGTON, D.C.

AND DISTRIBUTED BY THE
UNIVERSITY PRESS OF VIRGINIA
CHARLOTTESVILLE

1992

An exhibition at the
NATIONAL PORTRAIT GALLERY
SMITHSONIAN INSTITUTION
September 11, 1992, through February 7, 1993

Christman, Margaret C. S.
The spirit of party: Hamilton and Jefferson at odds /
Margaret C. S. Christman
p.   cm.
"An exhibition at the National Portrait Gallery, September 11,
1992, through February 7, 1993"—T.p. verso.
Includes bibliographical references and index.
ISBN 0-8139-1423-X
1. United States—Politics and government—1789-1797—
Exhibitions. 2. United States—Politics and government—
1789-1801—Exhibitions. 3. Political parties—United States—
History—18th century—Exhibitions. 4. Jefferson, Thomas,
1743-1826—Exhibitions. 5. Hamilton, Alexander, 1757-1804 —
Exhibitions. I. National Portrait Gallery
(Smithsonian Institution) II. Title.
E311.C477   1992
973.4'074753—dc20   92-19240   CIP

Cover illustrations

ALEXANDER HAMILTON (1755–1804)
By John Trumbull (1756–1843)
Oil on canvas, 1806
National Portrait Gallery, Smithsonian Institution;
gift of Henry Cabot Lodge

THOMAS JEFFERSON (1743–1826)
By Gilbert Stuart (1755–1828)
Oil on panel, 1805
National Portrait Gallery, Smithsonian Institution,
and Monticello; gift of the Regents of the Smithsonian
Institution, the Thomas Jefferson Memorial Foundation,
and the Enid and Crosby Kemper Foundation

CONTENTS

—

FOREWORD

The celebration of the 250th anniversary of the birth of Thomas Jefferson is surely an appropriate subject for national attention, and the National Portrait Gallery is glad to offer this book—and the exhibition to which it relates—as its part of this jubilee. Jefferson's role in writing the draft of the Declaration of Independence, participating in the discussions over the form of the new nation, negotiating with foreign governments as secretary of state, and—as President—enlarging the boundaries of the United States to the West and South surely constitute a contribution far beyond the call of duty. He has captured the imagination of our generation through his creative work in architecture, his pioneering planning of the University of Virginia, and his explorations in agronomy.

Jefferson has been remembered in earlier events with almost complete adulation, and no doubt many of the other books and exhibitions being presented on this anniversary will take a comparably celebratory view of this notable early citizen. But it bears remembering that Jefferson's life did not take place in a political vacuum. For practically every view he propounded, a contrary view also existed, and these were often defended with force and intelligence by his opponents. Therefore, this essay on Jefferson's view of the nation is being presented in the context of the political conflicts of his time.

The principal opponent of Jefferson's view of the state was Alexander Hamilton. The Hamiltonians viewed Jefferson's approach as overly favoring rural America, with its dependence upon market restraints, reliance upon slave labor, and weakening of the central government through excessive favoring of the rights of the states. Many northerners felt that Jeffersonian governance fostered dependence and lawlessness, "governed by coercion and the party spirit" (to quote Forrest McDonald), but Jefferson's view prevailed, especially in the South, until the Civil War forced the issue. McDonald believes that Hamilton's lack of prominence in comparison with Jefferson resulted from the fact that "most of American history was written by New England Yankees who, except for descendants of John Adams, almost uniformly idolized" Jefferson.

Whether or not this is the case, the essay in this book is intended to present both views in tandem, to suggest something of the nature of the political contest that raged in the final decade of the eighteenth century as these two powerful leaders and their followers contended for the leadership of the nation. These debates are by no means remote to our own times. As this is being written, the contest for the American presidency is more complex than it has been for more than seventy-five years, and the "Spirit of Party" is undergoing close scrutiny by the public and candidates alike. Newspaper columnists like George F. Will and aspirants to candidacy like Pat Buchanan have invoked Jefferson in support of their opinion that political freedom involves specific limitations on the power of central government. Others, however, such as Hamilton biographer Robert A. Hendrickson, have asserted that Hamiltonianism, as well, is needed as "a beacon of freedom and financial success in the modern world. It has peacefully discredited agrarianism, communism, and totalitarianism" (letter to the *Washington Post* on January 28, 1991).

So this is not just a bit of dry history, but a collision of views underlying American politics today. That Margaret Christman should have entitled her book "The Spirit of Party" instead of "The Spirit of Partisanship" is to suggest that these ideas created two enduring coalitions—two political poles that have remained powerful magnets for both theorists and practical politicians for almost two hundred years.

Wholly consistent with its approach, the National Portrait Gallery has centered this exhibition around images of individuals. This is particularly relevant here, since the central subjects and their associates are such compelling personalities. Jefferson himself believed in the importance of portraiture as historical documentation. He wrote to Joseph Delaplaine (May 3, 1789) that "our country should not be without the portraits of its first discoverers," and doubtless would have expanded this charge to other early national leaders. While the National Portrait Gallery is fortunate in possessing a number of the portraits of the significant players in this political drama, this book and exhibition could not have taken place without the generous cooperation of the many individuals who have loaned their precious possessions and the institutions that have made important objects available to us. We are deeply grateful for their participation.

ALAN FERN
Director, National Portrait Gallery

LENDERS TO THE EXHIBITION

Albany Institute of History and Art, New York
American Antiquarian Society, Worcester, Massachusetts
The Baltimore Museum of Art, Maryland
The Colonial Williamsburg Foundation, Virginia
Duke University, Durham, North Carolina
The Gibbes Museum of Art, Charleston, South Carolina
The Historical Society of Pennsylvania, Philadelphia
Independence National Historical Park Collection, Philadelphia, Pennsylvania
Kramer Gallery, Inc., St. Paul, Minnesota
The Library Company of Philadelphia, Pennsylvania
Library of Congress, Washington, D.C.
A. Theodore Lyman
Massachusetts Historical Society, Boston
The Metropolitan Museum of Art, New York, New York
Monticello, Charlottesville, Virginia
National Archives, Washington, D.C.
National Portrait Gallery, Smithsonian Institution, Washington, D.C.
New Jersey Historical Society, Newark
The New-York Historical Society, New York
The New York Public Library, New York
Peter B. Olney and Amy Olney Johnson
Lockwood Rush
The White House, Washington, D.C.
Yale University Art Gallery, New Haven, Connecticut

PROLOGUE

In March 1790, Thomas Jefferson arrived in New York to assume his duties as secretary of state and to encounter for the first time the secretary of the treasury, Alexander Hamilton. Differing in background, disposition, political philosophy, and public policy, the two were natural antagonists. Hamilton spoke to energy in government; Jefferson to the limits of government. Hamilton drove hard for federal authority; Jefferson insisted upon the prerogatives of the states. Hamilton dreaded anarchy; Jefferson feared tyranny. Hamilton was the champion of the moneyed interest, merchants, and speculators; Jefferson was the champion of the agrarian interest, "the chosen people of God."

Thomas Jefferson, son of a planter and surveyor, was born in the Virginia Piedmont to a well-established family. He entered the College of William and Mary, subsequently studied law, and began his political career with election to the House of Burgesses in 1769. Even before his marriage to the widowed Martha Wayles Skelton in 1772—a union that augmented his inheritance of land and slaves but also brought him the heavy burden of his father-in-law's English debts—Jefferson had embarked upon one of the great passions of his life, the building of the mountaintop house he called Monticello.

Alexander Hamilton came into the world on the British Island of Nevis in the West Indies, the "bastard Bratt of a Scotch Pedlar." Abandoned by his father, young Hamilton made his way, after the death of his mother, as a clerk in a St. Croix mercantile firm engaged in trade with New York. In 1772, the publication of his description of a dreadful August hurricane prompted several islanders to arrange for the furthering of his education in North America. While still a student at King's College (now Columbia), Hamilton took up his ever-ready pen in defense of the Continental Congress's boycott of British goods.

Whereas Jefferson, innately the political philosopher, labored for the patriotic cause at the Second Continental Congress and won immortal fame with his draft of the Declaration of Independence, Hamilton, with his bent for soldiering, served as an aide to General George Washington during the Revolutionary War. Finally given an independent command, he found glory in the capture of an enemy redoubt at the Battle of Yorktown.

Colonel Hamilton, whose 1780 marriage

ALEXANDER HAMILTON (1755–1804) by John Trumbull (1756–1843). Oil on canvas, 1806.
National Portrait Gallery, Smithsonian Institution; gift of Henry Cabot Lodge

THOMAS JEFFERSON (1743–1826) by Gilbert Stuart (1755–1828). Oil on panel, 1805. National Portrait Gallery, Smithsonian Institution, and Monticello; gift of the Regents of the Smithsonian Institution, the Thomas Jefferson Memorial Foundation, and the Enid and Crosby Kemper Foundation to General Philip Schuyler's daughter, Elizabeth, had brought him into the ranks of the New York aristocracy, left the army to study law and in 1782 undertook a frustrating stint as a member of the Confederation Congress, a body with no independent source of revenue.

Because of the delicacy of his wife's health, Thomas Jefferson declined appointment as one of the commissioners sent to bring an end to the war with England, but after her death in 1782 he sailed to France to conduct commercial negotiations and was shortly appointed minister to that country. In France, Hamilton noted, Jefferson "drank deeply of the French Philosophy, in Religion, in Science in Politics." He returned to America in 1789 after a six-year absence—years in which America had endured the impotency of government under the loose confederation of sovereign states—with a flush of exhilaration over the French Revolution for liberty and equality.

Meanwhile, Alexander Hamilton, in close collaboration with James Madison, drew up the call for a meeting of the states to consider how to strengthen the national government. At the ensuing Philadelphia Convention in 1787, Hamilton declared that "the British Govt. was the best in the world: and that he doubted much whether any thing short of it would do in America." Nevertheless, he was indefatigable in the fight for ratification of the Constitution, calling upon Madison and John Jay to unite with him in explaining and defending it through the essays that became known as the Federalist Papers.

As the government under the new Constitution was launched, Alexander Hamilton and Thomas Jefferson were called together as President George Washington's chief officers and soon found themselves "daily pitted in the cabinet like two cocks."

ENCOUNTER AT THE FIRST CONGRESS

—

*"My official labours so far have not
been unsuccessful."*
Alexander Hamilton to Angelica Schuyler Church,
January 31, 1791

By the time Thomas Jefferson arrived in the capital city of New York to take up his duties as secretary of state, Secretary of the Treasury Alexander Hamilton, whose comprehensive report on the public credit was before the Congress, was well entrenched as the dominant member of Washington's administration.

Ten days after Jefferson's arrival, the French chargé, Louis Guillaume Otto, summed up the new secretary. "In respect to resources, wealth, science, friendliness, and good dispositions toward Americans, he puts France above all other nations and he never wearies in praising her or in drawing true and lively pictures of Britain's prejudices, of her pride and vainglory, and of her animosity toward Americans."

If the French diplomat had cause enough to be pleased with Thomas Jefferson, British agent George Beckwith had equal cause to be pleased with Alexander Hamilton. "I have always preferred a Connexion with you, to that of any other Country," Hamilton told Beckwith in October 1789. "*We think in English*, and have a similarity of prejudices and of predilections." The secretary

of the treasury, all too ready to circumvent the secretary of state and intermeddle in foreign affairs, indicated to Beckwith that he wished to be kept apprised of any difficulties that might arise between their two countries "in order that I may be sure they are clearly understood, and candidly examined."

Toward the major controversy before the Congress—Hamilton's plan for funding the national debt and assuming the wartime debts of the states—Jefferson was at first conciliatory. Despite his concern that the adoption of Hamilton's program would mean that the national government would levy taxes better laid by state governments, Jefferson acknowledged the necessity of meeting the urgent demands of public creditors—particularly in Massachusetts and South Carolina—"for the sake of union, and to save us from the greatest of all calamities, the total extinction of our credit in Europe."

Writing, apparently, in 1792, Jefferson described how he had played a part in the Great Compromise of 1790, which had settled the two vexing issues that had brought Congress to a deadlock—assumption of state debts and the government's place of residence. "Going to the President's one day I met Hamilton as I approached the door. His look was sombre, haggard, and dejected beyond description. Even his dress uncouth and neglected. He asked to speak with me." A discouraged Hamilton, who had impressed upon Jefferson the indispensability of assumption to his fiscal program and its necessity to the preservation of the union, concluded that if he could not secure passage of the measure, "he could be of no use, and was determined to resign." He went on to solicit the secretary of state's help in bringing around his Virginia friends, whose fierce resistance to assumption arose in part because the state had made headway in paying its own debts. Jefferson responded by inviting Hamilton and James Madison to dinner, and an agreement was forged. It was arranged that votes would be secured for the passage of assumption, in return for the agreement to move the capital to Philadelphia for ten years and hence to a permanent location on the Potomac River—this last a measure that Jefferson and Madison had very much at heart.

Jefferson, greatly disturbed by the heavy speculation in government loan certificates —particularly the involvement by members of Congress, which he believed influenced them to vote in their own self-interest— now perceived assumption to be "a principal ground whereon was reared up that Speculating phalanx in and out of Congress." He would soon protest to President Washington that he had been duped by the secretary of the treasury, "and made a tool for forwarding his schemes, [which were] not then sufficiently understood by me."

During the last session of the First Congress—meeting now in Philadelphia— a fundamental difference arose over Hamilton's proposal for a Bank of the United States, which was modeled after the Bank of England. Jefferson, in agreement with Madison, maintained that the power to establish such an institution had not been given to Congress and urged that the President veto the legislation. "In the question concerning the Bank," Hamilton would later complain of Jefferson, "he not only delivered an opinion in writing against its constitutionality & expediency; but he did it *in a stile and manner* which I felt as partaking of asperity and ill humour towards me." For his part, Hamilton challenged Jefferson's strict construction of the Constitution by arguing that Congress had the implied power to do what was right and necessary to carry out its enumerated powers. President Washington signed the bank bill on February 25, 1791.

Differences between the two secretaries came to public attention with the publication in 1791 of Jefferson's "Report on Fisheries," which spoke to a favored treatment for French commerce and retaliation against the British, a course that would directly undermine the Treasury's dependence upon revenues from British trade. The foreign-policy views of Jefferson and Madison, Hamilton protested in a letter to Virginia Superintendent of Revenue Edward Carrington, were "unsound & dangerous. *They have a womanish attachment to France and a womanish resentment against Great Britain.*"

With the passage of an excise tax to generate the revenues necessary to carry out the obligations incurred by the funding and assumption bills, Hamilton was satisfied that the public credit was on a firm foundation. "My official labours so far have not been unsuccessful," he wrote to his sister-in-law Angelica Schuyler Church as the First Congress approached its close, "though they have not issued exactly as I wished, but *it is said* much better than could reasonably have been expected." Mrs. Church, who had been

GIRARD'S BANK, LATE THE BANK OF THE UNITED STATES, IN THIRD STREET PHILADELPHIA by
William R. Birch (1755–1834). Engraving, 1800. The Historical Society of Pennsylvania

a member of Thomas Jefferson's "charming coterie" in Paris, had the rare distinction of enjoying a particular friendship with both of the great antagonists.

Hamilton's financial program—deliberately fashioned to cement men of means to the new government—made the secretary of the treasury the hero of the hour among merchants and money men in the commercial North. Congressman Fisher Ames of Massachusetts, Hamilton's alter ego, applauding that the debt had been honored, the rights of property held sacred, and a revenue secured, enthusiastically declared, "I respect, I can almost say, I love our Secretary." The Bank of the United States was a particular source of satisfaction. "The eagerness to subscribe," Ames told Hamilton, "is a proof of the wealth and resources of the country and of the perfect confidence reposed by our opulent men in the Govt. People here are full of exultation and gratitude." To agrarian Jeffersonians, however, the Bank of the United States, whose eight-million-dollar public stock offering was avidly traded, was seen as having been designed "to serve the few, to encourage the undeserving speculator, and to undermine the republican principles."

"Are the people in your quarter," Jefferson inquired of Robert R. Livingston of New York, "as well contented with the proceed-

Angelica Church's portrait hung in the Schuyler house in Albany, and Alexander Hamilton playfully wrote to his sister-in-law that he had the pleasure of *dining in the presence of a lady for whom I have a particular friendship. I was placed directly in front of her and was much occupied with her during the whole Dinner. She did not appear to her usual advantage, and yet she was very interesting. The eloquence of silence is not a common attribute of hers.*

ANGELICA SCHUYLER CHURCH (1756–1815) with her child and servant by John Trumbull (1756–1843). Oil on canvas, circa 1785. Peter B. Olney and Amy Olney Johnson

ings of our government, as their representatives say they are? There is a vast mass of discontent gathered in the South."

Two months after the March 3, 1791, adjournment of the First Congress, Jefferson and Madison journeyed through New York, Vermont, and Connecticut, investigating flora and fauna, but also surely testing public opinion along the way. During their brief stop in New York City, the travelers met with Chancellor Robert R. Livingston, whose failure to gain a post in the Washington administration had curdled his Federalist sentiments, and with Aaron Burr, whom Livingston had recently helped to elect as senator from New York in place of Alexander Hamilton's father-in-law, Philip Schuyler. "There was every appearance of a passionate courtship between the Chancellor—Burr, Jefferson & Madison when the two latter were in town," Hamilton heard from his King's College classmate Robert Troup. The motto of destruction—"Delenda est Carthago"—"I suppose is the Maxim adopted with respect to you." Troup added, "Upon this subject however I cannot say that I have the smallest uneasiness. You are too well seated in the hearts of the citizens of the Northern & Middle States to be hunted down by them."

Massachusetts Congressman Fisher Ames, a fervent advocate of Hamilton's financial program, was characterized by Jefferson as "the colossus of the monocrats and paper men." On his part, Ames countered Republican charges that congressional votes were influenced by speculation with the assertion that "the Massachusetts members do not draw income enough merely from funded stock to buy the oats for the southern members' coach-horses."

FISHER AMES (1758–1808) by Gilbert Stuart (1755–1828). Oil on panel, circa 1807. National Portrait Gallery, Smithsonian Institution; gift of George Cabot Lodge

Although Mr. Madison "is a clever man, he is very little acquainted with the world," Alexander Hamilton told British agent George Beckwith, as Madison early showed himself in opposition to what Hamilton referred to as "my administration."

JAMES MADISON (1751–1836) by Gilbert Stuart (1755–1828). Oil on canvas, 1804. The Colonial Williamsburg Foundation

CONFRONTATION

====

*"The spirit of party has grown to
maturity sooner in this country than perhaps was
to have been counted upon."*
Alexander Hamilton to William Short,
February 5, 1793

Soon after the convening of the Second Congress in early December 1791, Alexander Hamilton issued his "Report on Manufactures." Most disturbing to Jefferson was the secretary of the treasury's advocacy of subsidies for the encouragement of infant industries. A horrified Jefferson, who saw Hamilton construing the power of the federal government to be all-encompassing, sought a private meeting with the President to insist that the authority to dispense bounties had not been delegated to the national government. To Jefferson, it was no less a question than "whether we live under a limited or an unlimited government." The matter remained moot, as Congress failed to take action on the report, but the conflict between Hamilton and Jefferson had intensified.

To Virginian Edward Carrington, Alexander Hamilton voiced his disillusionment with Congressman James Madison, whose firm support he had expected "in the *general course* of my administration." Although Madison had in fact offered serious challenge to Hamilton's financial program prior to Jefferson's arrival in New York—sponsoring unsuccessful legislation to give original

holders of government certificates a share in the redemption, and pressing for French commercial advantage—Hamilton blamed his defection on Jefferson's influence.

Hamilton was exasperated at the two Virginians' persistent efforts "to narrow the Federal authority," having persuaded themselves "that there is some dreadful combination against State Government & republicanism; which according to them, are convertible terms." Whereas, Hamilton went on to Carrington, "the *great* and *real* anxiety is to be able to preserve the National from the too potent and counteracting influence" of the state governments. He swiftly concluded of Jefferson, "I read him upon the whole thus—'A man of profound ambition & violent passions.'" Hamilton continued, "'Tis evident beyond a question, from every movement, that Mr Jefferson aims with ardent desire at the Presidential Chair."

There was no doubt in Jefferson's mind that two distinct parties had been formed—Republicans, who comprised the entire body of landholders and laborers, and Antirepublicans, by which he meant Hamilton's Federalist supporters. The first were more numerous, but the latter, since they all lived in the cities together, "give chief employment to the newspapers, & therefore have most of them under their command."

Jefferson acutely felt the need of a newspaper to counter John Fenno's pro-administration *Gazette of the United States*, which he characterized as "a paper of pure Toryism, disseminating the doctrines of monarchy, aristocracy, and the exclusion of the influence of the people." To facilitate national exposure to the Republican viewpoint, as well as to provide foreign news copied from the *Leyden Gazette*, rather than from the British press, Jefferson hired Philip Freneau as State Department translator and encouraged him to establish the *National Gazette*.

The pages of the *National Gazette*, which began publication in October 1791, were soon replete with criticism of the secretary of the treasury. One author who signed himself "Brutus" summed up: *It does not appear to me to be a question of* federalism *or* antifederalism: *but it is* the Treasury of the United States against the people.... *The influence which the treasury has on our government is truly alarming; it already forms a center, around which our political system is beginning to revolve.*

To Hamilton the *National Gazette* was clearly "a paper devoted to the subversion of me & the measures in which I have had an Agency." Writing anonymously in the *Gazette of the United States*, Hamilton began a series of personal attacks—under varying signatures—upon Jefferson, making him out to be an "ambitious incendiary, who would light a torch to the ruin of his country." The newspaper assault on the secretary of state, which had been devised to force him out of office, turned out to have the opposite effect. Although Jefferson had intended to retire at the end of George Washington's first term, his friends had persuaded him that

resignation "would injure me in the eyes of the public, who would suppose I either withdrew from investigation, or because I had not tone of mind sufficient to meet slander."

President Washington, the nation's symbol of unity, found the "newspaper squabbling between two public ministers" unexpected and distressing. "I would fain hope," he wrote to Hamilton on August 26, 1792, "that liberal allowances will be made for the political opinions of one another; and instead of those wounding suspicions, and irritating charges, with which some of our Gazettes are so strongly impregnated... there might be mutual forbearances and temporizing yieldings *on all sides.*" To Jefferson, Washington argued, "If, instead of laying our shoulders to the machine after measures are decided on, one pulls this way and another that, before the utility of the thing is fairly tried, it must, inevitably, be torn assunder."

Hamilton protested to the President that "I consider myself as the deeply injured party." He elaborated, *I know that I have been an object of uniform opposition from Mr. Jefferson, from the first moment of his coming to the City of New York to enter upon his present office. I know, from the most authentic sources, that I have been the frequent subject of the most unkind whispers and insinuating from the same quarter. I have long seen a formed party in the Legislature, under his auspices, bent upon my subversion.*

Jefferson, in his reply to the President on September 9, declared *that I have utterly, in my private conversations, disapproved of the system of the Secretary of the treasury, I acknolege and avow: and this was not merely a speculative difference. His system flowed from principles adverse to liberty, and was calculated to undermine and demolish the republic, by creating an influence of his department over the*

"I regret, deeply regret, the difference in opinions which have arisen and divided you and another principal officer of the Government," President George Washington wrote to Thomas Jefferson. "I have a great, a sincere esteem for you both."

GEORGE WASHINGTON (1732–1799) by Gilbert Stuart (1755–1828). Oil on canvas, 1797. (Once owned by Alexander Hamilton.) The New York Public Library, Astor, Lenox and Tilden Foundations

With good cause was South Carolina Congressman William Loughton Smith cited by the secretary of the treasury as "truly an excellent member—a ready clear speaker of a sound analytic head and the justest views." Commenting on Smith's oration in opposition to Madison's proposal for commercial retaliation against Britain, Jefferson remarked, "I am at no loss to ascribe Smith's speech to it's true father. Every tittle of it is Hamilton's except the introduction."

WILLIAM LOUGHTON SMITH (1758–1812) by Gilbert Stuart (1755–1828). Oil on canvas, circa 1795. The Gibbes Museum of Art, Carolina Art Association Collection

members of the legislature. Jefferson vigorously denied Hamilton's charges that he shrank from settling the national debt. *No man is more ardently intent to see the public debt soon & sacredly paid off than I am. This exactly marks the difference between Colo. Hamilton's views & mine, that I would wish the*

debt paid tomorrow; he wishes it never to be paid, but always to be a thing wherewith to corrupt and manage the legislature.

The next month Jefferson stopped by Mount Vernon to personally warn President Washington about Hamilton, relating that he had heard the secretary of the treasury say "that this constitution was a shilly shally thing of mere milk and water, which could not last, and was only good as a step to something better."

At almost the same moment, Hamilton observed in a letter concerning the approaching presidential election, "There was a time when I should have ballanced between Mr. Jefferson & Mr. Adams, but I now view the former as a man of sublimated & paradoxical imagination—cherishing notions incompatible with regular and firm government."

The Hamiltonians clearly defined Jefferson, rather than Madison—the Republican pilot in the House of Representatives—as the leader of the Republican party. Jefferson was the "Generalissimo," and Madison, second in command, the "General," as South Carolina Congressman William Loughton Smith put it in *Politicks and Views of a Certain Party*, published in the fall of 1792. Jefferson, according to Smith, was promoting his presidential ambitions "by decorating himself in the modest garb of pure Republicanism" and "by endeavoring to persuade his fellow citizens that they were miserable, and that the secretary of the treasury was the author of their misery." Jefferson, "setting no bounds to his ungovernable ambition follows up his object with anxious strides." Whereas Hamilton, claimed Smith, "unjustly" had "been deemed the ambitious competitor to higher honors."

In February 1793, near the end of the Second Congress, Representative William

Branch Giles of Virginia, with Jefferson's support behind the scenes, introduced a series of resolutions demanding a detailed accounting of the activities of the Treasury Department. "The spirit of party," Hamilton observed as he undertook the formidable task of answering the congressional challenge, "has grown to maturity sooner in this country than perhaps was to have been counted upon."

To the astonishment of the Republicans, who were sure that there would be no time to prepare a reply before Congress adjourned in early March, Hamilton came back with seven lengthy reports covering the whole history of his administration. Giles, undeterred, went ahead with nine resolutions of condemnation drafted by Jefferson but drew back from offering the tenth, which asked for the secretary's removal from office. On every count presented, Hamilton was exonerated by a large majority, owing, Jefferson was convinced, to the composition of the present House of Representatives, *one third of which is understood to be made up of bank directors & stock jobbers who would be voting on the case of their chief: and another third of persons blindly devoted to that party, of persons not comprehending the papers, or persons comprehending them but too indulgent to pass a vote of censure.*

Not until the arrival of the Swiss-born Albert Gallatin would Republicans have an authority who could challenge Hamilton in the field of finance. "If mr. Gallatin," Jefferson noted to Madison, would *present us with a clear view of our finances, & put them into a form as simple as they will admit, he will merit immortal honor. The accounts of the US. ought to be, and may be, made, as simple as those of a common farmer, and capable of being understood by common farmers.*

Gallatin subsequently published *A Sketch*

Albert Gallatin, a Genevan of aristocratic background, was derided by the Federalists as a foreigner who spoke with a French accent. But in Gallatin, who would succeed Madison as leader of the Republicans in the House of Representatives, the Jeffersonians at last had a financial mind who could offer challenge to Alexander Hamilton's method of operations.

ALBERT GALLATIN (1761–1849) by Gilbert Stuart (1755–1828). Oil on canvas, circa 1803. The Metropolitan Museum of Art; gift of Frederic W. Stevens, 1908

of the Finances of the United States, which confirmed Jefferson's belief that the national debt had been increasing at the rate of a million dollars a year and made the claim that Hamilton, in assuming the debts at random instead of carefully computing the amounts, had squandered about eleven million dollars.

French Minister Citizen Genet, fearful that he would lose his head under the Jacobin regime that had come to power in France, never returned to his country. He married Cornelia Clinton, daughter of the Antifederalist governor of New York, and settled down as an American farmer.

EDMOND CHARLES GENET (1763–1834) by Ezra Ames (1768–1836). Oil on panel, circa 1809–1810. Albany Institute of History and Art; bequest of the George Clinton Genet estate

ECHOES OF THE REVOLUTION IN FRANCE

*"There is no real resemblance between what was
the cause of America & what is the cause of France....
The difference is no less great than that
between Liberty & Licentiousness."*

Alexander Hamilton, May 18, 1793

The radical and violent turn of events in France had not quelled Thomas Jefferson's enthusiasm for "so beautiful a revolution." Writing in January 1793, he observed, *the liberty of the whole earth was depending on the issue of the contest, and was ever such a prize won with so little innocent blood? My own affections have been deeply wounded by some of the martyrs to this cause, but rather than it should have failed, I would have seen half the earth desolated.*

Alexander Hamilton saw it very differently. "The cause of France is compared with that of America during its late revolution," he wrote with indignation. "I acknowlege ... I am glad to believe, there is no real resemblance between what was the cause of America & what is the cause of France.... The difference is no less great than that between Liberty & Licentiousness."

Word of the beheading of King Louis XVI reached Philadelphia in mid-March, and soon thereafter came the news that France had declared war on England. On April 8 Citizen Edmond Charles Genet, the first minister from the Republic of France, ar-

Federalists were horrified by the beheading of Louis XVI, but popular sentiment remained strongly in favor of the Republic of France.

MASSACRE OF THE FRENCH KING! VIEW OF LA GUILLOTINE; OR THE MODERN BEHEADING MACHINE, AT PARIS. Broadside, 1793. Rare Books and Special Collections Division, Library of Congress

rived in Charleston, South Carolina. Washington summoned his cabinet to consider Genet's reception and to determine what policy America should pursue in regard to the warring powers.

29^d April 1793.

By the PRESIDENT of the United States of America.

A PROCLAMATION.

WHEREAS it appears that a ſtate of war exiſts between Auſtria, Pruſſia, Sardinia, Great-Britain, and the United Netherlands, of the one part, and France on the other, and the duty and intereſt of the United States require, that they ſhould with ſincerity and good faith adopt and pur-ſue a conduct friendly and impartial toward the belligerent powers:

I have therefore thought fit by theſe preſents to declare the diſpoſition of the United States to obſerve the conduct aforeſaid towards thoſe powers reſpectively; and to exhort and warn the citizens of the United States care-fully to avoid all acts and proceedings whatſoever, which may in any manner tend to contravene ſuch diſpoſition.

And I do hereby alſo make known that whoſoever of the citizens of the United States ſhall render himſelf liable to puniſhment or forfeiture under the law of nations, by committing, aiding or abetting hoſtilities againſt any of the ſaid powers, or by carrying to any of them thoſe articles, which are deemed contraband by the *modern* uſage of nations, will not receive the pro-tection of the United States, againſt ſuch puniſhment or forfeiture: and fur-ther, that I have given inſtructions to thoſe officers, to whom it belongs, to cauſe proſecutions to be inſtituted againſt all perſons, who ſhall, within the cognizance of the courts of the United States, violate the Law of Nations, with reſpect to the powers at war, or any of them.

IN TESTIMONY WHEREOF *I have cauſed the Seal of the United States of America to be affixed to theſe preſents, and ſigned the ſame with my hand. Done at the city of Philadelphia, the twenty-ſecond day of April, one thou-ſand ſeven hundred and ninety-three, and of the Independence of the United States of America the ſeventeenth.*

(L.S.)

G⁰. WASHINGTON.

By the President.

TH: JEFFERSON.

PRESIDENT GEORGE WASHINGTON'S PROCLAMATION OF NEUTRALITY, April 22, 1793.
National Archives

It was agreed by all that Genet should be received without condition, but Hamilton questioned the validity of the 1778 Treaty of Alliance, made with a now deposed and de-capitated monarch, and proposed that it should be suspended. Jefferson shot back that treaties were made between nations and not between rulers. The President put the matter off for further discussion.

All assented that a proclamation should be issued "declaring that we were in a state of peace with all the parties." Attorney Gen-eral Edmund Randolph drew it up, avoiding the word "neutrality," in deference to Jeffer-son's contention that such an assertion did not fall within the authority of the Presi-dent. "The public, however, soon took it up as a declaration of neutrality," Jefferson con-ceded, "and it came to be considered at length as such."

To James Madison, who regarded the proclamation as a virtual repudiation of America's alliance with France, Jefferson wrote, "I fear that a fair neutrality will prove

765

(154)

Philadelphia, Auguſt, 1793.

ALL able bodied ſeamen who are willing to engage in the cauſe of Liberty, and in the ſervice of the French Republic, will pleaſe to apply to the French Conſul, at No. 132, North Second-ſtreet.

Particular attention will be paid to the generous and intrepid natives of Ireland, who, it is preſumed, will act like thoſe warlike troops from that oppreſſed country, who took refuge in France about a century ago, and performed prodigies of valor under the old government of that country.

Theſe, and volunteers from any other country, will be received into preſent pay, and comfortable accommodations.

N. B. The Republic has, at this preſent time, in her ſervice, officers and ſoldiers from every civilized country in Europe, and natives of America, who, in imitation of the heroes from France in the American revolution are a glory to themſelves, and an honour to the country which gave them birth.

Citizen Genet, openly defying the Washington administration's determination to take no part in the war between France and England, proceeded to recruit Americans to man ships that would set out from American ports to prey on British commerce.

ALL ABLE BODIED SEAMEN WHO ARE WILLING TO ENGAGE IN THE CAUSE OF LIBERTY. Broadside, August 1793, from the papers of Citizen Genet. Rare Books and Special Collections Division, Library of Congress

Artist John Trumbull, Jefferson's kindred spirit in Europe, but also the brother of a Federalist senator, had, upon his return to America, been drawn into administration circles.

JOHN TRUMBULL (1756–1843) self-portrait. Oil on canvas, circa 1802. Yale University Art Gallery; gift of Marshall H. Clyde, Jr.

a disagreeable pill to our friends, tho' necessary to keep us out of the calamities of a war."

As Citizen Genet moved in slow progression toward Philadelphia, he was given a tumultuous reception all along the way, and Jefferson saw his arrival as "occasion for the *people* to testify their affections without respect to the cold caution of their government." Genet, in brazen defiance of America's policy of neutrality, proceeded to solicit Americans to outfit and man privateers to prey upon British commerce. Soon it was bruited about in Philadelphia that the French envoy had declared "that he would appeal from the President to the people."

The French minister "renders my position immensely difficult," Jefferson sighed to Madison. *Never in my opinion, was so calamitous an appointment made. . . . Hot headed, all imagination, no judgment, passionate disrespectful & even indecent towards the P[resident]. in his written as well as verbal communications, talking of appeals from him to Congress, from them to the people, urging the most unreasonable & groundless propositions, & in the most dictatorial style etc. etc. etc.*

On August 1, 1793, the cabinet unanimously agreed that Genet's recall should be requested. Jefferson confessed that he had been under a cruel dilemma in regard to the French minister. "I adhered to him as long as I could have a hope of getting him right," he apprised Madison. "Finding at length that the man was absolutely incorrigible, I saw the necessity of quitting a wreck which could not but sink all who should cling to it."

Jefferson, even as he and Hamilton were "daily pitted in the cabinet like two cocks," kept up his friendship with Angelica Church. Her letter, he wrote in reply on June 7, 1793, had "served to recall to my mind remembrances which are very dear to it, and which often furnish a delicious resort from the dry and oppressive scenes of business. Never was any mortal more tired of these than I am."

Relations with another member of the "charming coterie" in Paris, however, could not surmount the acrimony of the times. Painter John Trumbull, whose intention to commemorate the stirring events of the American Revolution had received Jefferson's enthusiastic support, and whom Jefferson regarded as "one of the best men as well as greatest artists in the world," had, upon his return to America, been drawn into the Federalist camp. "In Europe I had been on terms of confidence with Mr. Jefferson," Trumbull related in his *Autobiography*, "but as the French revolution advanced, my whole soul revolted from the atrocities of France, while he approved or apologized for all. He opposed Washington—I revered him—and a coldness gradually succeeded."

Political passions were momentarily diverted when, in August of 1793, the yellow fever struck Philadelphia, and most business was at a standstill until the frosts of November finally quelled the disease. "Hamilton is ill of the fever as is said," Jefferson wrote to James Madison on September 8. *He had been miserable several days before from a firm persuasion he should catch it. A man as timid as he is on the water, as timid on horseback, as timid in sickness, would be a phaenomenon if the courage of which he has the reputation in military occasions were genuine.*

To Dr. Benjamin Rush it came to seem that the treatment of the disease was governed by the spirit of party. Upon Hamilton's recovery from the fever, he sent a letter to the press praising his friend Dr. Edward Stevens's West Indian prescription of quinine, wine, and cold baths, causing many to turn away from Dr. Rush's publicized treatment of extensive bleeding and mercurial purges. Had his own method, Dr. Rush complained, "been introduced by any other person than a decided Democrat and a friend of Madison and Jefferson, they would have met with less opposition from Colonel Hamilton." It was with satisfaction that Rush wrote on October 2, "Colonel Hamilton's remedies are now as unpopular in our city as his funding system is in Virginia or North Carolina."

In July 1793 Thomas Jefferson had notified Washington of his firm determination to resign his office, but at the President's request he agreed to stay on until the end of

Dr. Benjamin Rush of Philadelphia, already outraged that the secretary of the treasury's policies had benefited speculators, who grabbed up loan certificates from soldiers and widows at a fraction of their face value, could not fail to be incensed when he heard that Alexander Hamilton "still defends bark and the cold bath in the yellow fever, and reprobates my practice as obsolete in the West Indies."

DR. BENJAMIN RUSH (1745–1813) by Edward Savage (1761–1817). Oil on canvas, circa 1799. Lockwood Rush

December. Informing Mrs. Church of his impending retirement, he wrote, "I am then to be liberated from the hated occupations of politics, and to remain in the bosom of my family, my farm, and my books. I have my house to build, my fields to farm, and to watch for the happiness of those who labor for mine."

Hamilton also wished to leave public life, but before he could in good conscience desert his post, he would have to oversee both a foreign policy and a domestic crisis.

When the terms of the treaty that John Jay negotiated with the British were revealed, Republicans sent up the cry of "Damn John Jay! Damn every one that won't damn John Jay!! Damn every one that won't put lights in his windows and sit up all night damning John Jay!!!"

JOHN JAY (1745–1829) begun by Gilbert Stuart (1755–1828) and finished by John Trumbull (1756–1843). Oil on canvas, circa 1783 and circa 1804–1808. National Portrait Gallery, Smithsonian Institution

TO AVOID A
WAR WITH ENGLAND

———

"Hamilton is really a colossus to the antirepublican party.
Without numbers, he is an host within himself."
Thomas Jefferson to James Madison,
September 21, 1795

In the spring of 1794 Britain's seizure of American ships in defiance of the rights of neutrals, as well as continued violation of the terms of the 1783 peace treaty, brought tempers to a boiling point, and war threatened. Jefferson, at Monticello, was dismayed to hear "that a special mission to England is meditated, & H. the missionary. A more degrading measure could not have been proposed," he told James Monroe. Hamilton, however, much as he would have relished the opportunity to visit England and his dear sister-in-law, had withdrawn his own name from consideration, telling the President that Chief Justice John Jay "is the only man in whose qualifications for success there would be a thorough confidence."

The selection of the pro-English Jay, well known for his suspicion of the French—nourished during his experience in negotiating the treaty that had brought the Revolution to a close—was small consolation to Jefferson. It gave Jefferson further disquiet to learn that Hamilton had personally drawn up Jay's instructions.

On the domestic front, opposition to the unpopular excise tax on whiskey, which Hamilton had persuaded the Congress to enact in 1791, had bubbled into open rebellion in western Pennsylvania. During the fall of 1794, Hamilton rode out with Washington to quell the insurgents. "You must not take my being here for a proof that I continue a quixot," Hamilton wrote to Angelica Church. "In popular governments 'tis useful that those who propose measures should partake in whatever dangers they may involve."

By the time the large force of militia reached its objective, the rebellion had evaporated. Hamilton "must have his alarms, his insurrections and plots against the Constitution," Jefferson reflected to Monroe. "But it answered the favorite purposes of strengthening government & increasing public debt; &, therefore, an insurrection was announced and proclaimed, & armed against, but could never be found."

"You say I am a politician, and good for nothing," Alexander Hamilton wrote gaily to Mrs. Church on December 8, 1794. "What will you say when you learn that after January next, I shall cease to be a politician at all?" As Hamilton left office to return to his gainful law practice in New

York, however, he told the President, "I beg Sir that you will at no time have any scruple about commanding me."

Washington had need enough for Hamilton's counsel when the provisions of the treaty Jay had negotiated with England were revealed to the country in time for denunciation at the Fourth of July celebrations of 1795. "The cry against the treaty," Washington reported to Hamilton, "is like that against a mad dog." Hamilton, who tried to defend it at a public meeting in New York City, was greeted with "hissings, coughings, and hootings," and was bloodied by a stone.

Even Federalists were disappointed by the meager concessions Jay had obtained, particularly the negligible opening allowed to American trade. The western forts, still held by the British, were to be evacuated in one year's time; however, there was no reference to impressment of sailors or payment for the slaves taken away during the Revolution. For the duration of the war with France, Britain claimed the right to seize neutral ships carrying foodstuffs to their enemy.

A great hue and cry was raised by the Republicans, who condemned the treaty, as Jefferson expressed it, "as wearing a hostile face to France." To Jefferson the Jay Treaty—which might more correctly be called the Hamilton Treaty—was an "infamous act, which is really nothing more than a treaty of alliance between England & the Anglomen of this country against the legislature & people of the United States."

Under the signature of "Camillus," Alexander Hamilton undertook to rally merchants and others in support of the treaty. Jefferson, who consistently declined to write for publication, urged Madison to take up his pen in rebuttal, exclaiming, "Hamilton is really a colossus to the antirepublican party.

Without numbers, he is an host within himself." Despite the Republicans' efforts, on February 29, 1796, the treaty was proclaimed by the President. James Monroe, Albert Gallatin, and Aaron Burr, however, resolved that party resistance would continue.

In April 1796, Hamilton heard from Fisher Ames that House Republicans, meeting in a secret caucus, had agreed to block appropriations for the implementation of the treaty. "A most important crisis ensues," Hamilton wrote with urgency to his Federalist friends. "Great evils may result unless good men play their card well & with promptitude and decision. For we must seize and carry along with us the public opinion."

Hamilton himself rushed to declare in print that the Federal Convention had intended to vest treaty-making powers exclusively with the President and the Senate. Jefferson disagreed, privately asserting that the House of Representatives members "are perfectly free to pass the act or refuse it, governing themselves by their own judgment whether it is for good of their constituents to let the treaty go into effect or not."

Federalists, at Hamilton's urging, set about organizing meetings and starting petitions in favor of the treaty. Especially aggravating to the Jeffersonians was John Marshall's success in organizing a show of support at a Richmond meeting. President Washington would later testify to the efficacy of "the torrent of Petitions, and remonstrances which were pouring in from all the Eastern and middle States, and were beginning to come pretty strongly from that of Virginia."

Following prolonged debate—highlighted by Fisher Ames's emotional two-hour address, which brought a tear to every eye, said John Adams, "except some of the jackasses who had occasioned the necessity of the or-

Thomas Jefferson, aided by James Madison and Albert Gallatin, attempts to arrest the progress of the Federalist administration, as symbolized by the chariot drawn by President George Washington.

THE TIMES; A POLITICAL PORTRAIT by an unidentified artist. Hand-colored engraving, circa 1795. The New-York Historical Society

atory"—the House of Representatives on April 30, 1796, voted the appropriations necessary to conclude the treaty, leaving to the next administration the problem of dealing with French displeasure. "The Anglomen have in the end got their treaty through, and so far have triumphed over the cause of republicanism," Jefferson reflected to Monroe. "Yet it has been to them a dear bought victory. . . . They see that nothing can support them but the Colossus of the President's merits with the people, and the moment he retires, that his successor, if a Monocrat, will be overborne by the republican sense of his Constituents."

As early as February 1796, the Republicans had thought it "pretty certain that the president will not serve beyond his present

Abigail Adams, who, despite political differences, could never completely suppress her esteem for Thomas Jefferson, was under no illusions when it came to Alexander Hamilton.

ABIGAIL ADAMS (1744–1818) by Gilbert Stuart (1755–1828). Oil on canvas, 1800 (unfinished portrait). Massachusetts Historical Society

term." To James Monroe, Madison wrote in code, "The republicans knowing that Jefferson alone can be started with hope of success mean to push him."

On September 19 Washington's "Farewell Address," which Alexander Hamilton had put into final form, was published. The next day Madison advised Monroe, "I have not seen Jefferson and have thought it best to present him no opportunity of protesting to his friend against being embarked in the contest."

Thomas Jefferson did not shrink from the Republican nomination, and out of geographic considerations the Virginian was paired with New Yorker Aaron Burr. On the Federalist side, John Adams of Massachusetts, then the Vice President, ran with Thomas Pinckney of South Carolina, who had negotiated the Spanish treaty that gave Americans navigation rights on the Mississippi. Since the Constitution—until the ratification of the Twelfth Amendment in 1804—provided that electors vote separately for President and Vice President, all four men had a chance of coming in first or second, regardless of party.

Alexander Hamilton "publickly gave out his wishes that Pinckney should be elected President," from "an apprehension," James Madison suspected, that Adams "is too headstrong to be a fit puppet for the intriguers behind the skreen." Hamilton calculated that if New England held steady for both Federalist candidates, Pinckney, popular in the South, might be brought in first. It turned out that John Adams was the victor over Thomas Jefferson by three votes.

"You may recollect that I have often told you," Abigail Adams wrote to her husband in the wake of the election, "H. is a Man ambitious as Julius Ceaesar, a subtle intriguer. His abilities would make him more dangerous if he was to espouse a wrong side. His thirst for Fame is insatiable. I have ever kept my eye on him."

THE ADAMS ADMINISTRATION

——

"Party passions are indeed high."
Thomas Jefferson to James Madison,
May 3, 1798

Vice President Jefferson arrived in Philadelphia, ready to preside over the Senate but determined to take no part in the decisions of the executive department. "I cannot have a wish to see the scenes of 93 revived as to myself," he declared, recalling the heated cabinet meetings of the Washington administration, "& to descend daily into the arena like a gladiator to suffer martyrdom in every conflict."

And if Jefferson was now clearly the leader of the Republican party, Alexander Hamilton was the commanding presence among the Federalists and had every intention of exerting his influence on the Adams administration. This he was able to accomplish with ease, since the new President kept on Washington's cabinet—Timothy Pickering at State, Oliver Wolcott at Treasury, and James McHenry at War—all of whom looked to Hamilton for guidance.

Relations with France were at a crisis as the French Directory, affronted over the Jay Treaty, refused to receive the new American minister, Charles Cotesworth Pinckney. Hamilton, conscious that the United States was not prepared for war, wanted peace with France fully as much as Jefferson did. Know-ing that his advice would not be welcomed by President John Adams, Hamilton proposed, through several Federalists who had the President's ear, that a commission be sent to negotiate with the French Directory. Hamilton suggested Pinckney, combined with a known French partisan such as Jefferson or Madison, and—to provide a margin of safety—a reliable Federalist such as George Cabot of Massachusetts.

Hamilton likewise pressed his proposal upon Pickering, Wolcott, and McHenry, who were at first skeptical, but on March 31, 1797, Wolcott told his predecessor in confidence "that the President had determined on instituting a Commission, but it *would not have been composed as you now propose*." The President ultimately nominated Pinckney, Virginia Federalist John Marshall (who was Jefferson's cousin), and Adams's old friend Elbridge Gerry of Massachusetts.

President Adams in May called a special session of Congress—fulfilling another of Hamilton's recommendations and causing Jefferson to frown in disapproval—to urge that the country take measures to defend itself against hostile France. Hamilton made free with his advice to Secretary of War McHenry, insisting upon a vigorous increase

John Adams came to the presidency in 1797 with the uncomfortable knowledge that Alexander Hamilton, who had maneuvered to confine him to second place, was the man many Federalists regarded as the leader of their party.

JOHN ADAMS (1735–1826) by John Trumbull (1756–1843). Oil on canvas, 1793. National Portrait Gallery, Smithsonian Institution

An arch-Federalist in his politics, Secretary of State Timothy Pickering was a model of republican simplicity in his daily living. "I have odd, old-fashioned notions," he avowed. "Neither powder nor pomatum has touched my head this twelvemonth, not even to cover my baldness."

TIMOTHY PICKERING (1745–1829) by Gilbert Stuart (1755–1828). Oil on panel, 1808. A. Theodore Lyman

Oliver Wolcott, chosen by Alexander Hamilton to be second in command at the Treasury, became the secretary upon Hamilton's departure in January 1795. Wolcott, the British minister reported to his government, is "a very candid and worthy man, and much in Hamilton's confidence."

OLIVER WOLCOTT, JR. (1760–1833) by Gilbert Stuart (1755–1828). Oil on canvas, circa 1820. Yale University Art Gallery; gift of George Gibbs, M.A. (Hon.), 1808

PROPERTY PROTECTED, *a la Francoise.*

In this English cartoon satirizing the XYZ affair, the five members of the French Directory prepare to extort tribute from a lady symbolic of America.

PROPERTY PROTECTED, A LA FRANCOISE attributed to Ansell, pseudonym for Charles Williams (died after 1830). Colored engraving, 1798. Prints and Photographs Division, Library of Congress

of revenue, a naval force, and, as a substitute for a standing army, a provisional army of 25,000 men. "Make a last effort for peace but be prepared for the worst," Hamilton instructed.

In March 1798, Alexander Hamilton learned from Secretary of State Pickering that the American mission had been insulted by French agents identified as "X Y and Z," who demanded a bribe and a large loan for France as a condition for being received by foreign minister Talleyrand. Jefferson was not apprised of the matter.

Hamilton, delighted to hear that Republicans in Congress had demanded the communications from the envoys to France, urged Timothy Pickering to see that the papers be made public. On April 3 President Adams laid the diplomatic correspondence before Congress, and the Federalist Senate saw to its publication.

Jefferson thought to exonerate the French government by casting blame on Talleyrand, who as an émigré in Philadelphia had been on friendly terms with Alexander Hamilton. The envoys, Jefferson observed, *have been assailed by swindlers, whether with or without the participation of Taleyrand is not very apparent. The known corruption of his character renders it very possible he may have intended to share largely in the 50,000£ demanded. But that the Directory knew anything of it is neither proved or probable.*

"The Country is united in opposition to the measures of France & rises indignant with one voice," wrote Abigail Adams, repeating the toasts offered to John Marshall, the first of the envoys to return from France "'millions for defence, but not a cent for tribute.'" To Jefferson's discomfort, Congress approved a provisional army of ten thousand men, a navy, and increased taxes to pay for defense.

Young men pledged to defend the country against the French paraded the streets of Philadelphia with fifes and drums and nightly played "The Rogue's March" under Thomas Jefferson's windows. At public gatherings glasses were raised to "The Vice-President—May his heart be purged of Gallicism in the pure fire of Federalism or be lost in the furnace."

"Party passions are indeed high," Jefferson told Madison on May 3. "However, the fever will not last. War, land tax & stamp tax, are sedatives which must calm its ardor. They will bring on reflection, and that, with information, is all which our countrymen need, to bring themselves and their affairs to rights."

In the wake of the insulting demand for a bribe by the French agents identified as XYZ, John Marshall lost no time withdrawing from France, taking passage, he humorously noted, on the *Alexander Hamilton,* "a very excellent vessel but for the sin of the name which makes my return in her almost as criminal as if I had taken England in my way." The first of the three commissioners to arrive back in America, Marshall was treated as a great hero, cheered and feted everywhere he went.

JOHN MARSHALL (1755–1835) by Charles Balthazar Julien Févret de Saint-Mémin (1770–1852). Black and white chalk on paper, 1807–1808. Duke University; bequest of Edward C. Marshall

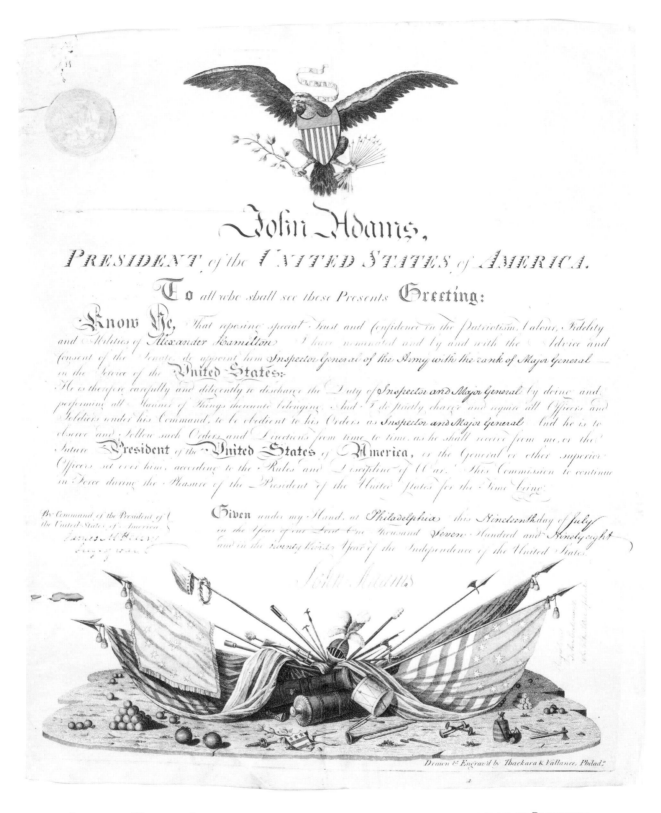

ALEXANDER HAMILTON'S COMMISSION AS INSPECTOR GENERAL OF THE ARMY, SIGNED BY PRESIDENT JOHN ADAMS, July 1798. Manuscripts Division, Library of Congress

THE QUASI-WAR
WITH FRANCE

====

"Can such an army under Hamilton be disbanded?"
Thomas Jefferson to Edmund Pendleton,
April 22, 1799

Alexander Hamilton was in a high state of alarm that England might be defeated by France, leaving America liable to Gallic invasion. He instructed Secretary of State Timothy Pickering, "Our duty our honor & safety require that we shall take vigorous and comprehensive measures of defence adequate to the immediate protection of our Commerce to the security of our Ports and to our eventual defence in case of Invas[ion]." Nothing did Hamilton have more at heart than that the President should proclaim a day of fasting, humiliation, and prayer. "It will be politically useful," Hamilton maintained, "to impress our nation that there is a serious state of things—to strengthen religious ideas in a contest which in its progress may require that our people may consider themselves as the defenders of their Country against Atheism conquest & anarchy."

As the nation prepared to defend "our fire sides & our altars" against France, Colonel Hamilton campaigned to be named second in command of the provisional army, just behind General Washington, who would not take the field except in case of invasion. Washington, manipulated by Timothy Pick-

ering and James McHenry, indicated to President Adams that Hamilton—Washington thought justifiably—would not make the sacrifice of coming into the army unless he was appointed second in rank. Colonel Hamilton, Washington conceded, is by some *considered an ambitious man, and therefore a dangerous one. That he is ambitious I shall readily grant, but it is of that laudable kind which prompts a man to excel in whatever he takes in hand. He is enterprising, quick in his perceptions, and his judgment intuitively great: qualities essential to a Military character, and therefore I repeat, that his loss will be irreparable.* To his great chagrin, John Adams found that he had no choice but to give Alexander Hamilton control of the provisional army.

"Can such an army under Hamilton be disbanded?" worried Jefferson. "Even if a H. of Repr. can be got willing & wishing to disband them? I doubt it, & therefore rest my principal hope on their inability to raise anything but officers." Such, indeed, proved to be the case, as recruitment lagged and was finally overtaken by events.

With the country in a state of undeclared war, the Congress passed two alien laws—aimed against Irish and French immigrants—and a sedition act aimed against Republican editors. Jefferson was gravely concerned. "I consider those laws as merely an experiment on the American mind," he wrote, *to see how far it will bear an avowed violation of the constitution. If this goes down we shall immediately see attempted another act of Congress, declaring that the President shall continue in office during life, reserving to another occasion the transfer of the succession to his heirs, and the establishment of the Senate for life.*

In concert with James Madison, who drew up resolutions to be acted upon by the Virginia General Assembly, Jefferson secretly drafted resolves to be submitted to the Kentucky legislature. These called upon the other states to associate themselves in opposition to the Alien and Sedition acts and declare them void. Any such action was seen by Hamilton as a threat far beyond any possible abuses engendered by the controversial laws. "The late attempt of Virginia & Kentucke to unite the state legislature in a direct resistance to certain laws of the Union," he proclaimed, "can be considered in no other light than as an attempt to change the Government."

The Sedition Act, which was intended to protect the President and Congress from abuse, afforded no relief to the Vice President. "Jefferson on his return home from the last sitting of Congress was indiscreet enough to accept of the honor of a public entertainment in Virginia on a *Sunday*," Robert Troup reported. "This fact has been trumpeted from one end of the continent to the other as an irrefragable proof of his contempt for the Christian religion and his devotion to the new religion of France." Jefferson observed to Elbridge Gerry that he had "been a constant butt for every shaft of calumny which malice & falsehood could

form, & the presses, public speakers, or private letters disseminate."

From various sources, including his son John Quincy Adams, who was minister to Berlin, President Adams became convinced that the French government would be receptive to a renewed overture for negotiations. To the "surprise, indignation, grief & disgust" of the Federalists, the President—without so much as consulting his cabinet—precipitously announced in February 1799 that he was appointing William Vans Murray, currently minister to the Hague, as minister to the French Republic.

If an accommodation with France was to be sought, Hamilton advised, the Federalists must insist on a three-man commission to undertake negotiations. This, indeed, Adams was forced to do, and Chief Justice Oliver Ellsworth as well as William R. Davie, Federalist governor of North Carolina, were to act with Murray.

To Jefferson's disappointment, Ellsworth and Davie were not to leave America until they obtained assurances that they would be received with respect by the French government. As it happened, with the President long absent in Massachusetts because of his wife's illness, his Hamiltonian cabinet managed to delay the departure of the envoys for nearly nine months.

Finally in October 1799 President Adams arrived in Trenton, where the government was meeting because of the yellow-fever epidemic in Philadelphia, and ordered that Ellsworth and Davie should embark for France. Hamilton, Adams later recalled, came to remonstrate against the departure of the mission, arguing that the monarchy would soon be restored to France. Hamilton spoke, remembered Adams, "with such agitation and violent action, that I really pitied him, instead of being displeased."

THE PROVIDENTIAL DETECTION

In the nick of time, the federal eagle prevents Thomas Jefferson from sacrificing the Constitution upon the "Altar of Gallic Despotism." The document labeled "Mazzei" refers to a letter that Jefferson wrote to his Italian friend Philip Mazzei, deploring "men who were Solomons in council, and Samsons in combat, but whose hair has been cut off by the whore England"—which the Federalists trumpeted as a pointed insult to Washington.

THE PROVIDENTIAL DETECTION by an unidentified artist. Engraving, circa 1800. The Library Company of Philadelphia

Disappointment loomed ahead for Alexander Hamilton at every turn. In December George Washington—"an Aegis very essential to me"—died, and John Adams made no move to appoint Hamilton as commander-in-chief of the provisional army. Some months later Congress suspended enlistments and shortly abolished the force altogether.

For his part, Thomas Jefferson was actively preparing for the election of 1800. "The engine is the press," he alerted James Madison. "Every man must lay his purse & his pen under contribution." "A little patience," Jefferson counseled his friends, "and we shall see the reign of witches pass over, their spells dissolved, and the people recovering their true sight, restoring their government to its true principles."

Son, grandson, and great-grandson of New England theologians, Aaron Burr had an impeccable heritage. Yet, from his first entrance into the political arena, most of his contemporaries viewed him with suspicion and distrust. "As a public man," Alexander Hamilton assessed, Burr "is one of the worst sort— a friend to nothing but as it suits his interest and ambition." Jefferson would come to describe Burr "as a crooked gun, or other perverted machine, whose aim or stroke you could never be sure of."

AARON BURR (1756–1836) by Gilbert Stuart (1755–1828). Oil on canvas, circa 1794. New Jersey Historical Society

THE ELECTION OF 1800

*"If we must have an enemy at the head of
the Government, let it be the one whom we can
oppose & for whom we are not responsible."*
Alexander Hamilton to Theodore Sedgwick,
May 10, 1800

Alexander Hamilton was well aware that a most dangerous combination was developing, an alliance between Virginia's Republicans and New York Republicans led by Aaron Burr. Nonetheless, during the crucial New York assembly elections in the spring of 1800, he let himself be outmaneuvered by Burr.

Burr was successful in persuading some of the most influential men in the state to offer their names to the voters, but he kept the Republican slate secret until it was too late for the Federalists—torn by "Jealousies & schisms"—to mount a team of competing stature.

Hamilton's subsequent exertions during the three-day election period—April 29 to May 1—going from polling place to polling place on a white horse and making a speech at each one, failed to overcome Burr's well-planned strategy. The Republicans carried all twelve city seats, giving them control of the lower house of the state legislature and thus insuring presidential electors who would vote for Thomas Jefferson. Burr, Jefferson acknowledged, "has certainly greatly merited of his country, & the Republicans in particular, to whose efforts his have given a chance of success."

To circumvent the election results, Hamilton proposed to Governor John Jay that he call the current Federalist-dominated legislature into session for the purpose of changing the method of choosing presidential electors. "The scruples of delicacy and propriety…ought to yield to the extraordinary nature of the crisis," he told the governor. "They ought not to hinder the taking of a *legal* and *constitutional* step, to prevent an *Atheist* in Religion and a *Fanatic* in politics from getting possession of the helm of the State." Jay ignored Hamilton's appeal, noting at the bottom of the letter, "Proposing a measure for party purposes wh. I think it wd. not become me to adopt."

On May 11 the Republican members of Congress meeting in Philadelphia unanimously chose Aaron Burr to be Thomas Jefferson's running mate.

Federalist congressmen meeting in caucus on May 3 had agreed—many with reluctance—to support President John Adams for another term in office and selected Charles Cotesworth Pinckney as his running mate. Just a few days later, Federalist irritation with the personality and policies of Adams intensified, as news came of his abrupt dismissal of Secretary of War James McHenry and Secretary of State Timothy

James McHenry, Hamilton's fellow aide to General Washington during the Revolution, became secretary of war in 1796. McHenry "is a man of honour and entirely trustworthy," Oliver Wolcott assessed. "He is also a man of sense, and delivers correct opinions when required, but he is not skilled in the details of Executive business, and he is at the head of a difficult and unpopular department." Aware of his own limitations, McHenry eagerly turned to Alexander Hamilton for detailed instructions.

JAMES MCHENRY (1753–1816) by James Sharples (1751–1811). Pastel on paper, circa 1796–1797. Independence National Historical Park Collection

Pickering. "You are subservient to Hamilton," Adams ranted to McHenry, "who ruled Washington, and would still rule if he could. Washington saddled me with three Secretaries who would controul me, but I shall take care of that."

By May, Hamilton had made up his mind to abandon Adams. "I will never more be responsible for him by my direct support," he declared, "even though the consequence should be the election of *Jefferson*. If we must have an *enemy* at the head of the Government, let it be the one whom we can oppose & for whom we are not responsible."

Hamilton's resentment of President John Adams was stoked by a letter from James McHenry, which quoted Adams as saying, "Hamilton is an intriguant—the greatest intriguant in the World—a man devoid of every moral principle—a Bastard, and as much a foreigner as Gallatin. Mr. Jefferson is an infinitely better man; a wiser one, I am sure, and, if President, will act wisely."

To promote the election of Pinckney and to vindicate his own character, Hamilton drew up a letter to be circulated among the Federalists—and which Aaron Burr made sure found its way into print—expounding at great length on John Adams's failures and foibles. Near the end of some fifty pages, Hamilton concluded that not a single vote should be withheld from Mr. Adams, but neither should a single vote be withheld from Pinckney.

"The influence . . . of this letter upon Hamilton's character is extremely unfortunate," his close friend Robert Troup assessed. "The federalists ask, what avail the most preeminent talents—the most distinguished patriotism—without the all important quality of discretion? Hence he is considered as an unfit head of the party—and we are in fact without a rallying point."

As far as the election was concerned, Hamilton's philippic had little effect—Federalists had known long since that the tide ran against them. "Have our party shown that they possess the necessary skill and courage to deserve to be continued to govern?" James McHenry reflected to Oliver Wolcott. "They write private letters. To whom? To each other. But they do nothing to give a proper direction to the public mind."

Resentment over increased taxation, and to a lesser extent the furor over the Alien and Sedition acts, had made the country ripe for change. Republicans were well organized to take advantage of the discontent, which they fueled through an expanded Republican press. Fisher Ames said afterward, "The newspapers are an overmatch for any Government.... The Jacobins owe their triumph to the unceasing use of this engine; not so much to skill in use of it, as by repetition."

The last remaining doubt about the defeat of John Adams and Charles Cotesworth Pinckney was resolved on December 2, 1800, after the electors in Pinckney's home state of South Carolina voted in lock step for Thomas Jefferson and Aaron Burr. "Such was the bitterness of party spirit," wrote South Carolina Congressman William Loughton Smith, "that one of the most distinguished citizens of America had not one vote in his own state."

When the electoral votes were counted, Jefferson and Burr had an equal number. "Mr. Hamilton has carried his eggs to a fine market," pronounced John Adams. "The very two men of all the world that he was most jealous of are now placed over him."

Burr did not unequivocally withdraw his name from contention, as expected, and Federalists in the House of Representatives—where an election resulting in a tie would be decided—schemed to make him President, "from the greater unfitness of Jefferson." In passionate dissent, Hamilton argued that "Burr, as President would disgrace our Country abroad. No agreement with him could be relied upon.... His ambition

Alexander Hamilton's most compelling arguments failed to convince Delaware Congressman James A. Bayard to vote for Thomas Jefferson, but he finally abandoned Aaron Burr, lest the nation be brought to chaos.

JAMES A. BAYARD (1767–1815) by Charles Balthazar Julien Févret de Saint-Mémin (1770–1852). Black and white chalk on paper, 1802. The Baltimore Museum of Art; bequest of Ellen Howard Bayard

aims at nothing short of permanent power and wealth in his own person. For heaven's sake let not the Foederal party be responsible for the elevation of this Man."

Attempting to sway James A. Bayard of Delaware, who alone would determine his state's vote, Hamilton wrote that it was too late for him to become Jefferson's apologist, nor did he have any disposition to do so. *I admit that his politics are tinctured with fanaticism, that he is too much in earnest in his democracy, that he has been a mischevous enemy to the principle measures of our past administration, that he is crafty & persevering in his objects, that he is not scrupulous about the means of success, nor very mindful of truth, and that he is a contemptible hypocrite. But it is not true as is alleged that he is an enemy to the power of the Executive, or that he is for confounding all the powers in House of Rs.* In a prophetic burst of insight, Hamilton observed that Jefferson "was generally for a large construction of the Executive authority, & not backward to act upon it in cases which coincided with his views."

Bayard, who thought of Hamilton as the Federalist party's "*Father confessor* in politics," nevertheless resisted Hamilton's counsel. "There would be really cause to fear that the government would not survive the course of moral & political experiments to which it would be subjected in the hands of Mr. Jefferson," he told Hamilton. On February 16, however, after staying with Burr through thirty-five ballots, the Delaware congressman "resolved not to risk the constitution or civil war," and announced his intention of voting for Jefferson. The next day Bayard, along with Federalists from South Carolina, Vermont, and Maryland, cast blank ballots, thus permitting Jefferson to come into the presidency.

EPILOGUE

"We are all republicans: we are all federalists," pronounced President Jefferson in his conciliatory inaugural address on March 4, 1801. In a private letter he explained, *I consider the pure federalist as a republican who would prefer a somewhat stronger executive; and the republican as one more willing to trust the legislature as a broader representation of the people, and a safer deposit of power for many reasons. But both sects are republican, entitled to confidence of their fellow citizens. Not so their quondam leaders, covering under the mask of federalism hearts devoted to monarchy.* First among these Jefferson named "the Hamiltonians."

Nonetheless, Hamilton's fiscal program stood. "We can pay off his debt in 15 years," Jefferson lamented, "but we can never get rid of his financial system."

In April of 1802, the President was dismayed to learn that Spain had surrendered its territory in Louisiana to France. In November the Spanish intendant, preparing for the French takeover, closed the port of New Orleans to American commerce.

Alexander Hamilton imagined Jefferson to be in a terrible dilemma. "The great embarrassment must be how to carry on war without taxes," Hamilton wrote. "Yet how is popularity to be preserved with the Western partisans if their interests are tamely sacrificed?" Hamilton avowed, "I have always held that the Unity of our empire and the best interests of our Nation require that we should annex to the UStates all the territory East of the Mississippi, New Orleans included."

New Orleans in the hands of an impetuous, energetic, and restless France, Jefferson acknowledged, would be an eternal source of irritation that would inevitably involve America in a war with their greatest friend. In January 1803 Jefferson appointed James Monroe to join the minister to France, Robert R. Livingston, for purposes of negotiating the purchase of New Orleans. Much to the astonishment of the Americans, Napoleon offered to sell the whole of the Louisiana Territory. Monroe and Livingston concluded the deal at a price of $15,000,000 for an area that would more than double the size of the United States.

It was now the Federalists' turn to deplore the increase in the national debt—Hamilton was almost alone among his party to applaud the purchase. "Louisiana, in open and avowed defiance of the Constitution, is to be added to the Union," Fisher Ames wrote

The Inaugural Speech of Thomas Jefferson.

WASHINGTON-CITY, MARCH 4th, 1801—THIS DAY, AT XII O'CLOCK,

THOMAS JEFFERSON,

PRESIDENT ELECT OF THE UNITED STATES OF AMERICA,

TOOK THE OATH OF OFFICE REQUIRED BY THE CONSTITUTION, IN THE SENATE CHAMBER, IN THE PRESENCE OF THE SENATE, THE MEMBERS OF THE HOUSE OF REPRESENTATIVES, THE PUBLIC OFFICERS, AND A LARGE CONCOURSE OF CITIZENS. PREVIOUSLY TO WHICH, HE DELIVERED THE FOLLOWING

ADDRESS:

Friends & Fellow-Citizens,

CALLED upon to undertake the duties of the first Executive Office of our country, I avail myself of the presence of that portion of my fellow-citizens which is here assembled, to express my grateful thanks for the favour with which they have been pleased to look towards me, to declare a sincere consciousness that the task is above my talents, and that I approach it with those anxious and awful presentiments which the greatness of the charge, and the weakness of my powers so justly inspire. A rising nation, spread over a wide and fruitful land, traversing all the seas with the rich productions of their industry; engaged in commerce with nations who feel power and forget right; advancing rapidly to destinies beyond the reach of mortal eye: when I contemplate these transcendent objects, and see the honor, the happiness, and the hopes of this beloved country committed to the issue and the auspices of this day, I shrink from the contemplation, and humble myself before the magnitude of the undertaking. Utterly indeed should I despair, did not the presence of many, whom I here see, remind me, that, in the other high authorities provided by our Constitution, I shall find resources of wisdom, of virtue, and of zeal, on which to rely under all difficulties. To you, then, gentlemen, who are charged with the sovereign functions of legislation, and to those associated with you, I look with encouragement for that guidance and support, which may enable us to steer with safety the vessel in which we are all embarked, amidst the conflicting elements of a troubled world.

DURING the contest of opinion through which we have passed, the animation of discussions and of exertions has sometimes worn an aspect which might impose on strangers unused to think freely, and to speak and to write what they think; but this being now decided by the voice of the nation, announced according to the rules of the Constitution, all will of course arrange themselves under the will of the law, and unite in common efforts for the common good. All too will bear in mind this sacred principle, that though the will of the majority is in all cases to prevail, that will, to be rightful, must be reasonable; that the minority possess their equal rights, which equal laws must protect, and to violate would be oppression. Let us then, fellow-citizens, unite with one heart and one mind; let us restore to social intercourse that harmony and affection, without which liberty, and even life itself, are but dreary things. And let us reflect, that having banished from our land that religious intolerance under which mankind so long bled and suffered, we have yet gained little, if we countenance a political intolerance, as despotic, as wicked, and capable of as bitter and bloody persecutions. During the throes and convulsions of the ancient world, during the agonising spasms of infuriated man, seeking through blood and slaughter his long lost liberty, it was not wonderful that the agitation of the billows should reach even this distant and peaceful shore; that this should be more felt and feared by some, and less by others; and should divide opinions as to measures of safety: but every difference of opinion is not a difference of principle. We have called by different names brethren of the same principle. We are all republicans: we are all federalists. If there be any among us who would wish to dissolve this Union, or to change its republican form, let them stand undisturbed as monuments of the safety with which error of opinion may be tolerated, where reason is left free to combat it. I know indeed that some honest men fear that a republican government cannot be strong; that this government is not strong enough. But would the honest patriot, in the full tide of successful experiment, abandon a government which has so far kept us free and firm, on the theoretic and visionary fear, that this government, the world's best hope, may, by possibility, want energy to preserve itself? I trust not. I believe this, on the contrary, the strongest government on earth. I believe it the only one, where every man, at the call of the law, would fly to the standard of the law, and would meet invasions of the public order as his own personal concern. Sometimes it is said that man cannot be trusted with the government of himself. Can he then be trusted with the government of others? Or have we found angels, in the form of kings, to govern him? Let history answer this question.

LET us then, with courage and confidence, pursue our own federal and republican principles; our attachment to union and representative government. Kindly separated by nature and a wide ocean from the exterminating havoc of one quarter of the globe; too high-minded to endure the degradations of the others; possessing a chosen country, with room enough for our descendants to the hundredth and thousandth generation; entertaining a due sense of our equal right to the use of our own faculties, to the acquisitions of our own industry, to honor and confidence from our fellow-citizens, resulting not from birth, but from our actions and their sense of them; enlightened by a benign religion,

professed indeed and practised in various forms, yet all of them inculcating honesty, truth, temperance, gratitude, and the love of man; acknowledging and adoring an over-ruling Providence, which, by all its dispensations, proves that it delights in the happiness of man here, and his greater happiness hereafter. With all these blessings, what more is necessary to make us a happy and a prosperous people? Still one thing more, fellow-citizens, a wise and frugal government, which shall restrain men from injuring one another, shall leave them otherwise free to regulate their own pursuits of industry and improvement, and shall not take from the mouth of labor the bread it has earned. This is the sum of good government; and this is necessary to close the circle of our felicities.

ABOUT to enter, fellow-citizens, on the exercise of duties which comprehend every thing dear and valuable to you, it is proper you should understand what I deem the essential principles of our government, and consequently those which ought to shape its administration. I will compress them within the narrowest compass they will bear, stating the general principle, but not all its limitations. Equal and exact justice to all men, of whatever state or persuasion, religious or political: peace, commerce, and honest friendship with all nations, entangling alliances with none: the support of the state governments in all their rights, as the most competent administrations for our domestic concerns, and the surest bulwark against anti-republican tendencies: the preservation of the general government in its whole constitutional vigour, as the sheet anchor of our peace at home, and safety abroad: a jealous care of the right of election by the people; a mild and safe corrective of abuses which are lopped by the sword of revolution, where peaceable remedies are unprovided: absolute acquiescence in the decisions of the majority, the vital principle of republics, from which is no appeal but to force, the vital principle and immediate parent of despotism: a well disciplined militia, our best reliance in peace, and for the first moments of war, till regulars may relieve them: the supremacy of the civil over the military authority: economy in the public expense, that labor may be lightly burthened: the honest payment of our debts, and sacred preservation of the public faith: encouragement of agriculture, and of commerce as its handmaid: the diffusion of information, and arraignment of all abuses at the bar of the public reason: freedom of religion; freedom of the press; and freedom of person, under the protection of the *habeas corpus*: and trial by juries impartially selected. These principles form the bright constellation, which has gone before us, and guided our steps through an age of revolution and reformation. The wisdom of our sages, and blood of our heroes, have been devoted to their attainment: they should be the creed of our political faith, the text of civic instruction, the touchstone by which to try the services of those we trust; and should we wander from them in moments of error or of alarm, let us hasten to retrace our steps, and to regain the road which alone leads to peace, liberty and safety.

I REPAIR, then, fellow-citizens, to the post you have assigned me. With experience enough in subordinate offices to have seen the difficulties of this, the greatest of all, I have learnt to expect that it will rarely fall to the lot of imperfect man to retire from this station with the reputation, and the favour, which bring him into it. Without pretensions to that high confidence you reposed in your first and greatest revolutionary character, whose pre-eminent services had entitled him to the first place in his country's love, and destined for him the fairest page in the volume of faithful history, I ask so much confidence only as may give firmness and effect to the legal administration of your affairs. I shall often go wrong through defect of judgment. When right, I shall often be thought wrong by those whose positions will not command a view of the whole ground. I ask your indulgence for my own errors, which will never be intentional; and your support against the errors of others, who may condemn what they would not, if seen in all its parts. The approbation implied by your suffrage, is a great consolation to me for the past; and my future solicitude will be, to retain the good opinion of those who have bestowed it in advance, to conciliate that of others, by doing them all the good in my power, and to be instrumental in the happiness and freedom of all.

RELYING then on the patronage of your good will, I advance with obedience to the work, ready to retire from it whenever you become sensible how much better choices it is in your power to make. And may that Infinite Power, which rules the destinies of the universe, lead our councils to what is best, and give them a favourable issue for your peace and prosperity.

Thomas Jefferson

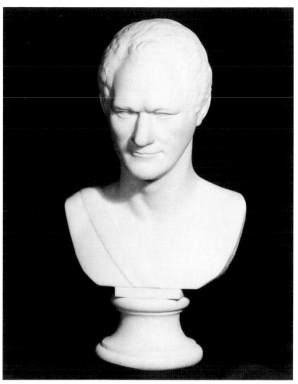

Thomas Jefferson, a great admirer of the classical past, suggested to Gilbert Stuart in 1805 that his head be taken "a la antique." The medallion profile, much esteemed by Jefferson and his family, was copied by Charles Bird King for Jefferson's granddaughter, Mrs. Nicholas Trist.

THOMAS JEFFERSON (1743–1826) by Charles Bird King (1785–1862), after Gilbert Stuart. Oil on panel, 1836. Kramer Gallery, Inc.

The Italian sculptor Giuseppe Ceracchi portrayed both Hamilton and Jefferson in Roman guise, but Jefferson's bust, which stood opposite Hamilton's at Monticello, was destroyed in the Library of Congress fire of 1851.

ALEXANDER HAMILTON (1755–1804) by Giuseppe Ceracchi (1751–1801/2). Marble, 1794 replica after 1791 original. National Portrait Gallery, Smithsonian Institution

in disapproval. Timothy Pickering, now a senator from Massachusetts, who dreaded that the states carved out of the huge territory would mean an inevitable ascendancy of the western and southern interests, was more active in his disapproval. It seemed to

"Printers have vied with each other in printing it upon Satin," Jefferson was told of his inaugural address, and window glass "used to set it in frames for parlours. Teachers in schools are causing the youths under their care to commit it to memory."

"THE INAUGURAL SPEECH OF THOMAS JEFFERSON." Broadside on silk, 1801. American Antiquarian Society

Pickering, and to a number of other New Englanders, that the only escape from Republican and slaveholding domination was a secession of the New England states, to be joined by New York. Pickering looked to Aaron Burr to help effect his scheme.

Burr, who had been replaced by George Clinton as the Republican vice-presidential candidate in the upcoming election of 1804, sought to become governor of New York, and Pickering promoted his election among New York Federalists. Were New York under a Burr administration, Pickering argued, "Jefferson would then be forced to observe some caution and forebearance in his measures. And if a *separation* should be deemed proper, the five New England States, New York and New Jersey would naturally be united."

Hamilton would have no part in disunion and, alarmed at any slight possibility of a Burr election, vigorously joined forces with his old foe, George Clinton, in support of the alternative Republican candidate, Morgan Lewis. Lewis won by a large margin.

After the election was over, Burr demanded an explanation for remarks reported in the press, that at an Albany dinner Hamilton had declared that he "looked upon Mr. Burr to be a *dangerous man,* and one *who ought not be trusted with the reins of Government.*" Hamilton, who could not deny his severe criticism of Burr's political principles and private conduct, felt that the only honorable course was to offer Burr satisfaction on the dueling ground.

On July 4, 1804, John Trumbull recorded in his memoirs, "I dined with the society of the Cincinnati, my old military comrades, and then met, among others, Gen. Hamilton and Col. Burr. . . . Hamilton entered with glee into all the gaiety of a convivial party, and even sung an old military song." One week later Hamilton received his mortal wound from Burr, and Trumbull reaped a harvest in a demand for posthumous portraits.

Jefferson made no more than a casual mention of Hamilton's death, but in the hall at Monticello, to the right of the door, he placed a bust of Alexander Hamilton; to the left he positioned his own image. "Opposed in death as in life," he was wont to tell visitors.

CHECKLIST OF THE EXHIBITION

THE WASHINGTON ADMINISTRATION, 1789-1797

ALEXANDER HAMILTON (1755–1804)
By John Trumbull (1756–1843)
Oil on canvas, 1806
76.2 × 60.9 cm. (30 × 24 in.)
National Portrait Gallery, Smithsonian
Institution; gift of Henry Cabot Lodge
Illustrated on page 12

THOMAS JEFFERSON (1743–1826)
By Gilbert Stuart (1755–1828)
Oil on panel, 1805
66.4 × 53.3 cm. (26⅛ × 21 in.)
National Portrait Gallery, Smithsonian
Institution, and Monticello; gift of the Regents
of the Smithsonian Institution, the Thomas
Jefferson Memorial Foundation, and the Enid
and Crosby Kemper Foundation
Illustrated on page 13

GEORGE WASHINGTON (1732–1799)
By Gilbert Stuart (1755–1828)
Oil on canvas, 1797
130.3 × 102.2 cm. (51⁵⁄₁₆ × 40¼ in.)
The New York Public Library, Astor, Lenox and
Tilden Foundations
Illustrated on page 23

FISHER AMES (1758–1808)
By Gilbert Stuart (1755–1828)
Oil on panel, circa 1807
76.2 × 63.5 cm. (30 × 25 in.)
National Portrait Gallery, Smithsonian
Institution; gift of George Cabot Lodge
Illustrated on page 19

JAMES MADISON (1751–1836)
By Gilbert Stuart (1755–1828)
Oil on canvas, 1804
74.3 × 60.9 cm. (29¼ × 24 in.)
The Colonial Williamsburg Foundation
Illustrated on page 20

WILLIAM LOUGHTON SMITH (1758–1812)
By Gilbert Stuart (1755–1828)
Oil on canvas, circa 1795
74.5 × 60.6 cm. (29⁵⁄₁₆ × 23⅞ in.)
The Gibbes Museum of Art, Carolina Art
Association Collection
Illustrated on page 24

GIRARD'S BANK, LATE THE BANK
OF THE UNITED STATES, IN THIRD
STREET PHILADELPHIA
By William R. Birch (1755–1834)
Engraving, 1800
21.6 × 28.6 cm. (8½ × 11¼ in.)
The Historical Society of Pennsylvania
Illustrated on page 17

ALBERT GALLATIN (1761–1849)
By Gilbert Stuart (1755–1828)
Oil on canvas, circa 1803
74.6 × 63.2 cm. (29⅛ × 24⅞ in.)
The Metropolitan Museum of Art; gift of
Frederic W. Stevens, 1908
Illustrated on page 25

GAZETTE OF THE UNITED STATES,
September 8, 1792 (facsimile of the front page)
Serial and Government Publications Division,
Library of Congress

THE NATIONAL GAZETTE, July 4, 1792
(facsimile of the front page)
Serial and Government Publications Division,
Library of Congress

ECHOES OF THE REVOLUTION IN FRANCE

MASSACRE OF THE FRENCH KING!
VIEW OF LA GUILLOTINE; OR THE
MODERN BEHEADING MACHINE, AT PARIS
Broadside, 1793
Rare Books and Special Collections Division,
Library of Congress
Illustrated on page 27

PRESIDENT GEORGE WASHINGTON'S
PROCLAMATION OF NEUTRALITY,
April 22, 1793
National Archives
Illustrated on page 28

EDMOND CHARLES GENET (1763–1834)
By Ezra Ames (1768–1836)
Oil on panel, circa 1809–1810
76.5 × 59.7 cm. (30⅛ × 23½ in.)
Albany Institute of History and Art; bequest of
the George Clinton Genet estate
Illustrated on page 26

ALL ABLE BODIED SEAMEN WHO
ARE WILLING TO ENGAGE IN THE CAUSE
OF LIBERTY
Broadside, 1793
Rare Books and Special Collections Division,
Library of Congress
Illustrated on page 29

THE TIMES; A POLITICAL PORTRAIT
By an unidentified artist
Hand-colored engraving, circa 1795
31.1 × 45.1 cm. (12¼ × 17¾ in.)
The New-York Historical Society
Illustrated on page 35

TO AVOID A WAR WITH ENGLAND

JOHN JAY (1745–1829)
Begun by Gilbert Stuart (1755–1828) and finished
by John Trumbull (1756–1843)
Oil on canvas, circa 1783 and circa 1804–1808
128.3 × 101.6 cm. (50½ × 40 in.)
National Portrait Gallery, Smithsonian Institution
Illustrated on page 32

HAMILTON'S PERSONAL COPY OF *DEFENCE
OF THE TREATY . . . ENTERED INTO
BETWEEN THE UNITED STATES OF AMERICA
AND GREAT BRITAIN . . . UNDER THE
SIGNATURE OF CAMILLUS,* 1795
The New-York Historical Society

TIES OF FRIENDSHIP

DR. BENJAMIN RUSH (1745–1813)
By Edward Savage (1761–1817)
Oil on canvas, circa 1799
74.9 × 62.2 cm. (29½ × 24½ in.)
Lockwood Rush
Illustrated on page 31

JOHN TRUMBULL (1756–1843)
Self-portrait
Oil on canvas, circa 1802
76.2 × 63.5 cm. (30 × 25 in.) sight
Yale University Art Gallery; gift of Marshall H.
Clyde, Jr.
Illustrated on page 30

ANGELICA SCHUYLER CHURCH (1756–1815)
By John Trumbull (1756–1843)
Oil on canvas, circa 1785
92.1 × 71.1 cm. (36¼ × 28 in.)
Peter B. Olney and Amy Olney Johnson
Illustrated on page 18

THOMAS JEFFERSON (1743–1826)
By John Trumbull (1756–1843)
Oil on panel, not dated
12.1 × 7.6 cm. (4¾ × 3 in.)
The White House, on indefinite loan to the
National Portrait Gallery, Smithsonian Institution

THE ADAMS ADMINISTRATION, 1797–1801

JOHN ADAMS (1735–1826)
By John Trumbull (1756–1843)
Oil on canvas, 1793
65.1 × 54.6 cm. (25⅝ × 21½ in.)
National Portrait Gallery, Smithsonian Institution
Illustrated on page 38

ABIGAIL ADAMS (1744–1818)
By Gilbert Stuart (1755–1828)
Oil on canvas, 1800 (unfinished portrait)
56.5 × 46.7 cm. (22¼ × 18⅜ in.)
Massachusetts Historical Society
Illustrated on page 36

THOMAS JEFFERSON (1743–1826)
By Charles Bird King (1785–1862), after
Gilbert Stuart
Oil on panel, 1836
57.2 × 48.9 cm. (22½ × 19¼ in.)
Kramer Gallery, Inc.
Illustrated on page 53

OLIVER WOLCOTT, JR. (1760–1833)
By Gilbert Stuart (1755–1828)
Oil on canvas, circa 1820
Yale University Art Gallery; gift of George Gibbs,
M.A. (Hon.), 1808
Illustrated on page 39

TIMOTHY PICKERING (1745–1829)
By Gilbert Stuart (1755–1828)
Oil on panel, 1808
71.1 × 57.2 cm. (28 × 22½ in.)
A. Theodore Lyman
Illustrated on page 39

JAMES MCHENRY (1753–1816)
By James Sharples (1751–1811)
Pastel on paper, circa 1796–1797
22.9 × 17.8 cm. (9 × 7 in.)
Independence National Historical Park
Collection
Illustrated on page 48

THE XYZ AFFAIR

JOHN MARSHALL (1755–1835)
By Charles Balthazar Julien Févret de Saint-
Mémin (1770–1852)
Black and white chalk on paper, 1807–1808
52.1 × 39.4 cm. (20½ × 15½ in.)
Duke University; bequest of Edward C. Marshall
Illustrated on page 41

PROPERTY PROTECTED, A LA FRANCOISE
Attributed to Ansell, pseudonym for Charles
Williams (died after 1830)
Colored engraving, 1798
27.6 × 42.7 cm. (10⅞ × 16¹³⁄₁₆ in.)
Prints and Photographs Division, Library of
Congress
Illustrated on page 40

ALEXANDER HAMILTON'S COMMISSION AS
INSPECTOR GENERAL AND MAJOR OF THE
ARMY, SIGNED BY PRESIDENT JOHN ADAMS,
July 1798
Manuscripts Division, Library of Congress
Illustrated on page 42

THE ALIEN ACT
Broadside, June 22, 1798
Rare Books and Special Collections Division,
Library of Congress

JEFFERSON'S KENTUCKY RESOLUTIONS,
November 16, 1798
Jefferson Papers, Manuscripts Division, Library of
Congress

THE ELECTION OF 1800

AARON BURR (1756–1836)
By Gilbert Stuart (1755–1828)
Oil on canvas, circa 1794
76.8 × 63.5 cm. (30¼ × 25 in.)
New Jersey Historical Society
Illustrated on page 46

JAMES A. BAYARD (1767–1815)
By Charles Balthazar Julien Févret de Saint-
Mémin (1770–1852)
Black and white chalk on paper, 1802
54.6 × 38.1 cm. (21½ × 15 in.)
The Baltimore Museum of Art; bequest of Ellen
Howard Bayard
Illustrated on page 49

THE PROVIDENTIAL DETECTION
By an unidentified artist
Engraving, circa 1800
41.6 × 35.6 cm. (16⅜ × 14 in.)
The Library Company of Philadelphia
Illustrated on page 45

LETTER FROM ALEXANDER HAMILTON,
CONCERNING THE PUBLIC CONDUCT
AND CHARACTER OF JOHN ADAMS, 1800
Rare Books and Special Collections Division,
Library of Congress

LETTER FROM ALEXANDER
HAMILTON TO GOUVERNEUR MORRIS,
December 26, 1800
Manuscripts Division, Library of Congress

LETTER FROM THOMAS JEFFERSON TO
BENJAMIN RUSH, January 16, 1811
Manuscripts Division, Library of Congress

THE INAUGURAL SPEECH OF
THOMAS JEFFERSON
Broadside on silk, 1801
55.2 × 40 cm. (21¾ × 15¾ in.)
American Antiquarian Society
Illustrated on page 52

ALEXANDER HAMILTON (1755–1804)
By Giuseppe Ceracchi (1751–1801/2)
Marble, 1794 replica, after 1791 original
57.5 cm. (22⅝ in.)
National Portrait Gallery, Smithsonian Institution
Illustrated on page 53

NOTES ON SOURCES

The first phrase of the quotation is followed by its citation.

PROLOGUE

"The chosen people," Thomas Jefferson, *Notes on the State of Virginia*, ed. William Peden (Chapel Hill, N.C., 1955), p. 165. "Bastard Bratt," in Lester J. Cappon, ed., *The Adams-Jefferson Letters* (Chapel Hill, N.C., 1959), vol. 2, p. 354. "Drank deeply," in Harold C. Syrett *et al.*, eds., *The Papers of Alexander Hamilton* (26 vols.; New York, 1961–1979), vol. 11, p. 439 [hereafter cited as *PAH*]. "The British Govt.," *PAH*, vol. 4, p. 192. "Daily pitted in the cabinet," in Paul Leicester Ford, ed., *The Writings of Thomas Jefferson* (10 vols.; New York, 1892–1899), vol. 9, p. 273.

ENCOUNTER AT THE FIRST CONGRESS, 1790–1791

"In respect to resources," in Julian Boyd *et al.*, eds., *The Papers of Thomas Jefferson* (24 vols. to date; Princeton, N.J., 1950–), vol. 18, p. 534 [hereafter cited as *PTJ*]. "I have always preferred," *PAH*, vol. 5, p. 483. "In order that I may be sure," *PAH*, vol. 6, p. 497. "For the sake of union," *PTJ*, vol. 16, p. 537. "Going to the President's," *PTJ*, vol. 17, p. 205. "A principal ground," *ibid.*, p. 207. "And made a tool," *PTJ*, vol. 24, p. 352. "In the question concerning," *PAH*, vol. 11, p. 430. "Unsound & dangerous," *ibid.*, p. 439. "My official labours," *PAH*, vol. 7, p. 608. "I respect, I can almost say," in Winfred E. A. Bernhard, *Fisher Ames, Federalist and Statesman* (Chapel Hill, N.C., 1965), p. 176. "The eagerness to subscribe," *PAH*, vol. 8, p. 589. "To serve the few," *National Gazette*, March 15, 1792. "Are the people in your quarter," *PTJ*, vol. 19, p. 241. "There was every appearance," *PAH*, vol. 8, p. 478.

CONFRONTATION, 1791–1792

"Whether we live under," Ford, *Writings of Jefferson*, vol. 1, p. 176. "In the *general course*," *PAH*, vol. 11, p. 427. "To narrow the Federal authority," *ibid.*, p.

442. "Give chief employment," Ford, *Writings of Jefferson*, vol. 7, p. 48. "A paper of pure Toryism," *PTJ*, vol. 20, p. 416. "It does not appear to me," *National Gazette*, September 1, 1792. "A paper devoted to the subversion," *PAH*, vol. 11, p. 431. "Ambitious incendiary," *Gazette of the United States*, September 8, 1792, in *PAH*, vol. 12, p. 379. "Would injure me," Ford, *Writings of Jefferson*, vol. 6, p. 164. "Newspaper squabbling," *PTJ*, vol. 24, p. 387. "I would fain hope," *PAH*, vol. 12, p. 276. "If, instead of laying," in John C. Fitzpatrick, ed., *The Writings of George Washington from the Original Manuscript Sources, 1745–1799* (39 vols.; reprint; Westport, Conn., 1970), vol. 32, pp. 130–31. "I consider myself," *PAH*, vol. 12, pp. 347–48. "That I have utterly," *PTJ*, vol. 24, p. 353. "No man is more ardently," *ibid.*, p. 355. "That this constitution," *PTJ*, vol. 24, p. 435. "There was a time," *PAH*, vol. 12, p. 569. "By decorating himself," [William Loughton Smith], *The Politics and Views of a Certain Party, Displayed* (Philadelphia?, 1792), p. 29. "The spirit of party," *PAH*, vol. 14, p. 7. "One third of which," *ibid.*, p. 195. "If mr. Gallatin," in William T. Hutchinson *et al.*, eds., *The Papers of James Madison* (17 vols. to date; Chicago and Charlottesville, Va., 1962–), vol. 16, p. 250 [hereafter cited as *PJM*].

ECHOES OF THE REVOLUTION IN FRANCE, 1793–1794

"So beautiful a revolution," *PTJ*, vol. 22, p. 72. "The liberty of the whole earth," Ford, *Writings of Jefferson*, vol. 6, p. 154. "The cause of France," *PAH*, vol. 14, p. 473. "The public, however," Ford, *Writings of Jefferson*, vol. 6, p. 346. "I fear that a fair," *PJM*, vol. 15, p. 11. "Occasion for the *people*," *ibid.* "That he would appeal," *PAH*, vol. 15, p. 72. "Renders my position," *PJM*, vol. 15, p. 43. "I adhered to him," *ibid.*, p. 57. "Daily pitted in the cabinet," Ford, *Writings of Jefferson*, vol. 9, p. 273. "Served to recall," *ibid.*, vol. 6, p. 289. "One of the best men," *PTJ*, vol.

19, p. 330. "In Europe," in Theodore Sizer, ed., *The Autobiography of Colonel John Trumbull* (New Haven, Conn., 1953), p. 173. "Hamilton is ill," *PJM*, vol. 15, p. 104. "Been introduced by any other," in L. H. Butterfield, ed., *Letters of Benjamin Rush* (2 vols.; Princeton, N.J., 1951), vol. 2, p. 701. "Colonel Hamilton's remedies," *ibid.*, p. 692. "I am then to be liberated," Ford, *Writings of Jefferson*, vol. 6, p. 455.

TO AVOID A WAR WITH ENGLAND, 1794–1796
"That a special mission," Ford, *Writings of Jefferson*, vol. 6, p. 504. "Is the only man," *PAH*, vol. 16, p. 278. "You must not take," *PAH*, vol. 17, p. 340. "Must have his alarms," Ford, *Writings of Jefferson*, vol. 7, p. 16. "You say I am a politician," *ibid.*, p. 428. "I beg Sir," *PAH*, vol. 19, p. 236. "The cry against the treaty," *PAH*, vol. 18, p. 524. "As wearing a hostile face," Ford, *Writings of Jefferson*, vol. 7, p. 27. "Infamous act," *ibid.*, p. 40. "Hamilton is really a colossus," *PJM*, vol. 16, p. 88. "A most important crisis," *PAH*, vol. 20, pp. 112–13. "Are perfectly free," Ford, *Writings of Jefferson*, vol. 7, p. 68. "The torrent of Petitions," Fitzpatrick, *Writings of Washington*, vol. 35, p. 62. "Except some of the jackasses," John Adams to Abigail Adams, April 28, 1796, Adams Papers, Massachusetts Historical Society. "The Anglomen," Ford, *Writings of Jefferson*, vol. 7, p. 89. "Pretty certain," *PJM*, vol. 16, p. 232. "I have not seen Jefferson," *ibid.*, p. 404. "Publickly gave out," in Charles R. King, ed., *The Life and Correspondence of Rufus King* (6 vols.; New York, 1894–1900), vol. 2, p. 466. "An apprehension," *PJM*, vol. 16, p. 422. "You may recollect," Abigail Adams to John Adams, December 31, 1796, Adams Papers, Massachusetts Historical Society.

THE ADAMS ADMINISTRATION, 1797–1798
"I cannot have a wish," *PJM*, vol. 16, p. 473. "That the President had determined," *PAH*, vol. 20, p. 569. "Make a last effort," *ibid.*, p. 574. "Have been assailed by swindlers," Ford, *Writings of Jefferson*, vol. 7, p. 238. "The Country is united," Abigail Adams to John Quincy Adams, July 14, 1798, Adams Papers, Massachusetts Historical Society. "Party passions," Ford, *Writings of Jefferson*, vol. 7, p. 250.

THE QUASI-WAR WITH FRANCE, 1798–1799
"Our duty our honor," *PAH*, vol. 21, p. 365. "It will be politically useful," *PAH*, vol. 20, p. 545. "Considered an ambitious man," Fitzpatrick, *Writings of Washington*, vol. 36, pp. 460–61. "Can such an army," Ford, *Writings of Jefferson*, vol. 7, pp. 375–76. "I consider those laws," *ibid.*, p. 283. "The late

attempt," *PAH*, vol. 23, p. 600. "Jefferson on his return home," King, *Rufus King*, vol. 2, p. 432. "Been a constant," Ford, *Writings of Jefferson*, vol. 7, p. 325. "Surprise, indignation, grief & disgust," King, *Rufus King*, vol. 2, p. 551. "With such agitation," in Charles Francis Adams, ed., *The Works of John Adams, Second President of the United States* (10 vols.; Boston, 1850–1856), vol. 9, p. 255. "An Aegis very essential," *PAH* vol. 24, p. 155. "The engine is the press," Ford, *Writings of Jefferson*, vol. 7, p. 344. "A little patience," *ibid.*, p. 265.

THE ELECTION OF 1800
"Has certainly greatly merited," Ford, *Writings of Jefferson*, vol. 7, pp. 449–50. "The scruples of delicacy," *PAH*, vol. 24, p. 465. "Proposing a measure," *ibid.*, p. 467. "You are subservient," *ibid.*, p. 557. "I will never more," *ibid.*, p. 475. "Hamilton is an intriguant," *ibid.*, p. 557. "The influence," King, *Rufus King*, vol. 3, p. 359. "Have our party shown," in Bernard C. Steiner, *The Life and Correspondence of James McHenry* (Cleveland, Ohio, 1907), p. 462. "The newspapers are an overmatch," in Seth Ames, ed., *Works of Fisher Ames* (2 vols.; Boston, 1854), vol. 1, p. 294. "Such was the bitterness," in George C. Rogers, Jr., *Evolution of a Federalist: William Loughton Smith of Charleston (1758–1812)* (Columbia, S.C., 1962), p. 351. "Mr. Hamilton has carried," in Page Smith, *John Adams* (2 vols.; New York, 1962), vol. 2, p. 1053. "Burr, as President," *PAH*, vol. 25, p. 269. "I admit that his politics," *ibid.*, pp. 319–20. "*Father confessor,*" in Elizabeth Donnan, ed., *Papers of James A. Bayard, 1796–1815* (reprint; New York, 1971), p. 115. "There would be really cause," *PAH*, vol. 25, p. 301. "Resolved not to risk," Donnan, *Papers of Bayard*, pp. 126–27.

EPILOGUE
"I consider the pure federalist," Ford, *Writings of Jefferson*, vol. 8, p. 76. "We can pay off his debt," *ibid.*, p. 127. "The great embarrassment," *PAH*, vol. 26, pp. 71–72. "Louisiana, in open and avowed," in Charles Warren, *Jacobin and Junto: or Early American Politics as Viewed in the Diary of Dr. Nathaniel Ames, 1758–1822* (reprint; New York, 1968), p. 162. "Jefferson would then be forced," in Dumas Malone, *Jefferson the President* (Boston, 1970), p. 405. "Looked upon Mr. Burr," in Mary-Jo Kline, ed. *The Founding Fathers—Alexander Hamilton: A Biography in His Own Words* (New York, 1973), p. 398. "I dined with the society," Sizer, *John Trumbull*, pp. 237–38. "Opposed in death," in Fiske

Kimball, *The Life Portraits of Jefferson and Their Replicas* (Philadelphia, 1944), p. 514.

CAPTIONS

Angelica Schuyler Church: "Dining in the presence of a lady," *PAH*, vol. 24, p. 212.

Fisher Ames: "The colossus of the monocrats," Ford, *Writings of Jefferson*, vol. 6, p. 134. "The Massachusetts members," Ames, *Works of Fisher Ames*, vol. 1, p. 142.

James Madison: "Is a clever man," *PAH*, vol. 5, p. 488.

George Washington: "I regret," in Newsweek Books, ed., *The Founding Fathers—Thomas Jefferson: A Biography in His Own Words* (New York, 1974), p. 133.

William Loughton Smith: "Truly an excellent," *PAH*, vol. 12, p. 544. "I am at no loss," *PJM*, vol. 15, p. 301.

Dr. Benjamin Rush: "Still defends bark," in Butterfield, *Letters of Rush*, vol. 2, p. 738.

John Jay: "Damn John Jay!" in Frank Monaghan, *John Jay, Defender of Liberty* . . . (New York, 1935), p. 399.

Timothy Pickering: "I have odd," in Octavius Pickering, *The Life of Timothy Pickering* (4 vols.; Boston, 1867–1873), vol. 1, p. 215.

Oliver Wolcott: "A very candid and worthy," in Robert A. Hendrickson, *The Rise and Fall of Alexander Hamilton* (New York, 1981), p. 426.

John Marshall: "A very excellent vessel," in Charles T. Cullen *et al.*, eds., *Papers of John Marshall*, vol. 3 (Chapel Hill, N.C., 1979), p. 463.

The Providential Detection: "Men who were Solomons," Ford, *Writings of Jefferson*, vol. 7, p. 76.

Aaron Burr: "As a public man," *PAH*, vol. 12, p. 480. "As a crooked gun," Ford, *Writings of Jefferson*, vol. 9, p. 46.

James McHenry: "Is a man of honour," in George Gibbs, *Memoirs of the Administrations of Washington and John Adams, Edited from the Papers of Oliver Wolcott, Secretary of the Treasury* (2 vols.; New York, 1846), vol. 2, p. 315.

"The Inaugural Speech of Thomas Jefferson": "Printers have vied," in Merrill D. Peterson, *Thomas Jefferson and the New Nation* (New York, 1970), p. 659.

FOR FURTHER READING

———

Adams, Henry. *The Life of Albert Gallatin.* Reprint. New York, 1943.

Bowling, Kenneth R. "Dinner at Jefferson's: A Note on Jacob E. Cooke's 'The Compromise of 1790.'" *William and Mary Quarterly* 3d ser. 28 (October 1971): 630-40.

Bush, Alfred L. *The Life Portraits of Thomas Jefferson.* Charlottesville, Va., 1987.

Cooke, Jacob E. "The Compromise of 1790." *William and Mary Quarterly* 3d ser. 27 (October 1970): 523-45.

———. Rebuttal of "Dinner at Jefferson's: A Note on Jacob E. Cooke's 'The Compromise of 1790'" by Kenneth R. Bowling. *William and Mary Quarterly* 3d ser. 28 (October 1971): 640-48.

———. *Alexander Hamilton.* New York, 1982.

Cunningham, Noble E., Jr. *The Image of Thomas Jefferson in the Public Eye.* Charlottesville, Va., 1981.

Foley, John P., ed. *The Jeffersonian Cyclopedia.* 2 vols. Reprint. New York, 1967.

Kennedy, Roger G. *Orders from France: The Americans and the French in a Revolutionary World, 1780–1820.* New York, 1989.

McDonald, Forrest. *Alexander Hamilton.* New York, 1979.

Malone, Dumas. *Jefferson and His Time.* 6 vols. Boston, 1948-1981.

Miller, John C. *The Federalist Era, 1789-1801.* New York, 1960.

Mitchell, Stewart, ed. *New Letters of Abigail Adams, 1788–1801.* Boston, 1947.

Peterson, Merrill D. *Thomas Jefferson and the New Nation.* New York, 1970.

Rogers, George C., Jr. *Evolution of a Federalist: William Loughton Smith of Charleston (1758-1812).* Columbia, S.C., 1962.

Rutland, Robert Allen. *James Madison: The Founding Father.* New York, 1987.

Smith, Page. *John Adams.* 2 vols. New York, 1962.

William and Mary Quarterly. "James Madison, 1751-1836: Bicentennial Number." 3d ser. 8 (January 1951).

William and Mary Quarterly. "Alexander Hamilton, 1755-1804: Bicentennial Number." 3d ser. 12 (April 1955).

INDEX

Italicized page numbers refer to illustrations.

PHOTOGRAPHY CREDITS

WILL BROWN: page 31

GERALDINE T. MANCINI: page 30

ROLLAND WHITE: cover, pages 12, 13, 32, 38, 53

Edited by Frances K. Stevenson and Dru Dowdy

Designed by Gerard A. Valerio, Bookmark Studio, Annapolis, Maryland

Composed in Goudy Old Style by the Image Foundry, Baltimore, Maryland

Printed on one hundred-pound Karma by Schneidereith & Sons, Inc., Baltimore, Maryland